CLARITY BY DESIGN

COMPREHENSIVE CHECKLISTS
IN MEDICAL COMMUNICATION

KELLY SCHRANK

Copyright © 2025 Kelly Schrank

All rights reserved.

All trademarks are the property of their respective owners.

No portion of this book may be reproduced in any form without written permission from the publisher or author, except as permitted by U.S. copyright law.

This publication is designed to provide accurate and authoritative information in regard to the subject matter covered. It is sold with the understanding that neither the author nor the publisher is engaged in rendering legal, investment, accounting, or other professional services. While the publisher and author have used their best efforts in preparing this book, they make no representations or warranties with respect to the accuracy or completeness of the contents of this book and specifically disclaim any implied warranties of merchantability or fitness for a particular purpose. No warranty may be created or extended by sales representatives or written sales materials. The advice and strategies contained herein may not be suitable for your situation. You should consult with a professional when appropriate. Neither the publisher nor the author shall be liable for any loss of profit or any other commercial damages, including but not limited to special, incidental, consequential, personal, or other damages.

ISBN: 979-8-9932757-1-0

Edited by Christine McGeever

Cover and book design by CB Messer

Published by Bookworm Editing Services, LLC

DEDICATION

*To my husband, Chuck, whose patience
and encouragement made this possible.*

CONTENTS

INTRODUCTION 1
EXISTING LITERATURE 5
    The Checklist Manifesto: How to Get Things Right 5
    The Checklist Book: Set Realistic Goals, Celebrate Tiny Wins,
    Reduce Stress and Overwhelm, and Feel Calmer Every Day 6
    Listful Thinking: Using Lists to Be More Productive, Successful
    and Less Stressed 7
    "An Analysis of the Effectiveness of Checklists When Combined
    With Other Processes, Methods and Tools to Reduce Risk
    in High Hazard Activities" 8
BASIC VERSUS COMPREHENSIVE CHECKLISTS 11
WHO SHOULD USE CHECKLISTS? 13
WHY SHOULD YOU USE CHECKLISTS? 15
HOW DO YOU GET STARTED? 21
    1. Choose a task 21
    2. Document your actions 23
    3. Write down every step 24
    4. Type it into a file 25
    5. Add specifics 25
    6. Puts steps in the optimal order 26
    7. Add mechanics 28
    8. Add tracking items 30
    9. Test, revise, test, revise 32
    10. Use it! 32

CASE STUDY: MANUSCRIPT EDITING CHECKLIST 33
    Tracking Section 34
    First Pass Section 35
    Main Text Section 36
    Abbreviations Section 38
    References Section 38
    Author Instructions Section 40
    The Final Touches Section 40
    When Ready to Submit Section 41

HOW DO YOU KNOW YOU HAVE GOOD CHECKLISTS? 43

INTERVIEWS WITH CHECKLIST ENTHUSIASTS 47
    Interview with a Continuing Medical Education (CME) Writer and Checklist Enthusiast 47
    Interview with a Manuscript Editor and Checklist Enthusiast 55
    Interview with a Regulatory Writer and Checklist Specialist 62

SUMMARY 77

REFERENCES 79

CHECKLIST EXAMPLES 81
    Check Changes Checklist 82
    CME Writing Project Scope Checklist 84
    Dossier Checklist 88
    Financial Friday Checklist 92
    Manuscript Checklists 94
    Marketing Monday Checklist 103
    Slide Deck Checklists 106
    Speaking Engagements Checklist 110
    Standard Response Checklist 112
    YouTube Video Checklist 118

ABOUT THE AUTHOR 121

ACKNOWLEDGMENTS

Many thanks to the checklist users, fans, enthusiasts, and specialists whose dedication continues to demonstrate the value of this tool for medical communicators. Your commitment to clarity, precision, and excellence and your enthusiasm for checklists has directly influenced the development of this book. This work is for you.

INTRODUCTION

HOW A CHECKLIST SPECIALIST (AND A BOOK) WAS BORN

Before we get into how *you* can become a Checklist Specialist, I thought it might be helpful to discuss how *I* became a Checklist Specialist and came to write this book. Like many stories about the birth of a book, mine includes false starts and wrong turns, but years before I even thought about writing a book, I laid the groundwork to become a Checklist Specialist.

In 2010, I became a medical editor at a small company servicing a large pharmaceutical manufacturer. I had 14 years of experience as a technical editor, but I had never edited medical or pharmaceutical materials. As we started the project, the client provided a five-page multifunctional checklist meant to serve three audiences. At the time, I was trying to learn lots of new things at once and wanting desperately to please my employer and the client. And while I didn't know what I didn't know, it became clear to me that the checklist was sub-optimal. After hemming and hawing about how to make it work, I finally decided that the checklist was *not good*. It was too long and trying to be too many things for too many people. There had to be a better way!

Given my process-oriented nature and natural inclination for research, I tried to research how to make that bad checklist better, but the options were limited, either nonexistent or as bad as the one I had. If you search on the internet for checklists, you'll be inundated with options that don't tell you how to create your own checklists:

they are checklists for a task that someone has put together, often with no actual place for your checkbox and no action-oriented steps to be completed in order to earn the right to add your checkmark to the checkbox. I looked in my technical editing and technical writing textbooks, and the checklists were similarly basic. While they might be helpful to someone who is just starting out, they just seemed to be a start. I needed more.

As I found what little information was available (see the *Existing Literature* chapter), I began to create better checklists for myself, and later for the team that we gathered over time at that job. I talked to others about checklists. The first place I facilitated a discussion about checklists was at the American Medical Writers Association (AMWA) Conference in 2011. I gave a breakfast roundtable called *Using Checklists for More Efficient Editing*, which I repeated in 2012 and 2013, culminating in an invitation to do a journal article about it for the *AMWA Journal* in 2013 titled *Using Editing Checklists for More Efficient Editing* (it's still available online; see the *References* chapter).

In the intervening 12 years, I have talked about checklists online and in person as webinars, sessions, progressions, roundtables, spotlight talks, and workshops for many local and national groups related to my professional homes: AMWA, the Association of Independent Information Professionals (AIIP), the Board of Editors in the Life Sciences (BELS), the Editorial Freelancers Association (EFA), Editors Canada, the Society for Technical Communication (STC—now defunct), and private groups.

Working with a business coach (hey, Barb Stone!) from 2020 to 2022 (virtually), we decided that I needed to write a book. We even wrote a "contract" so that I could get out of my own way and stop selfishly keeping the content to myself. It was a simple contract, and it came with a reminder that said, "YOU HAVE A CONTRACT TO WRITE A BOOK FOR THE REST OF THE WORLD!" Yes, it was in ALL CAPs to show how important it was, but it still took a few years to make progress. At some point, I gathered the information from my talks into one place, almost a book form, but it was rough and tumble, nothing publishable.

And then again, it was Barb Stone who pushed me forward. I ran into her at a holiday party in December 2024, where she told me about a book she was having published. All our talk about me writing a book, and she was going to publish before me! We got together for coffee in January 2025 to catch up and discuss her progress, but I knew she also meant this to be a push to get me moving in the right direction on my own book even if she was no longer my business coach.

The conversation with Barb started a chain of events. Barb introduced me to Avril King, who was helping Barb with her book. Avril introduced me to Laura Thorne, co-owner of Wildebeest Publishing Company. Laura met with me every couple of weeks to set goals and make sure I made progress toward the completion of the book. Without her and pre-readers like Alexandra Howson, Angela Trenkle Hansen, Barb Stone, Chris Faison, Crystal Herron, and Sherri Henkin, I would not have continued moving forward. And near the end of the project, I reconnected with Christine McGeever, who gave it the thorough edit it needed after I had been looking at it for too long! And the absolute last person to touch the book was CB Messer, who is a fabulous cover designer and book designer. Seeing her creative work alongside my more technical content really made it come alive, which was very motivating for me to get this over the finish line!

While I initially talked about editing checklists for medical editors, in the intervening years, I have also discussed the use of checklists by other types of communicators, such as technical writers and editors, speakers, business owners, infopreneurs, and others. There might be more books in the future, but the microbook in your hand today will go back to my roots and focus on the use of comprehensive checklists for tasks in medical communication. Use it to create your own comprehensive checklists and become a Checklist Specialist in your work.

Kelly Schrank
Checklist Specialist

EXISTING LITERATURE

As someone in medical communication, you expect a discussion of the existing literature in any new topic, and checklists are no exception. But it's difficult to find books or even articles in journals about checklists in editing or writing tasks.

The best you can do is find content that discusses the use of checklists in workplaces or generic productivity concepts and adapt that to fit the work of medical communicators.

See the *References* chapter of this book for publisher information about the literature discussed here.

THE CHECKLIST MANIFESTO: HOW TO GET THINGS RIGHT

This is the ultimate checklist book. Any random internet article on checklists references this bestseller and seminal work from 2010. Atul Gawande, a well-known staff writer for *The New Yorker* and author of many bestsellers, wrote a whole book on how checklists are used by people in a variety of industries to save lives, fly planes, and manage large-scale construction projects. It covers checklists as people use them in the workplace, though it doesn't get specific to tasks that you are likely to do as medical communicators.

This book is a fun read; it has a running story about using checklists to save lives in operating rooms. It also dives into research about how other industries use checklists. From aviation to project management to investing, smart people in many industries use checklists to be more efficient and consistent and to help them make better decisions in their work lives.

There's much to take away from this book, but one of Gawande's most important points is when he talks about how people think using a checklist is beneath them because they're too smart to need that type of crutch. Consider this: maybe you don't need a checklist on your good days at work, when you've gotten enough sleep, when you have no worries occupying your mind, when you have no interruptions, and when you're in a great mood. But what about those days when one of those things, or all of those things, are off? The checklist is there for you, to make you be your better self, every day.

THE CHECKLIST BOOK: SET REALISTIC GOALS, CELEBRATE TINY WINS, REDUCE STRESS AND OVERWHELM, AND FEEL CALMER EVERY DAY

This is a newer addition to the checklist scene, published in 2020. While not directly related to what we do as medical communicators, the author Alexandra Franzen has some good advice and her own perspective. She understands many of the reasons for using checklists, believes in the power of a checklist, and has her own way of "doing" checklists—what she calls the Franzen Checklist Method.

In her introduction, she likens her book to a yoga class, and she advises readers to "take what you need" from the book, just like you would a yoga class. This is a great way to think about reading a book and what you should take away from a book, including readers of this book! Not everything in it will be pertinent to you and your work, but when you find something that resonates, take it and make it your own!

Like a yoga class, she refers to the process as such: "Making a checklist brings a little calm, focus, and meaning to the madness." She also refers to *The Checklist Manifesto* and the idea of checklists as "absurdly simple" tools that actually work. She points out that thinking that checklists are unnecessary because we will remember something is a strategy that rarely works out!

Other advantages of checklists, according to Franzen (and others), are that checklists feel rewarding (and our brain loves rewards) and reduce decision fatigue because the checklist takes us from unlimited options to just the items right here on this list.

Franzen discusses the origin of the checkmark itself. She believes the checkmark dates to the Roman Empire, where the letter "V" stood for "veritas" or "truth." Folks would put a V next to something to indicate it was "truly done" or "the complete truth." Over time, the V transformed to the checkmark symbol we use now. That's also a nice way to think about a checkmark's place in your work: when it's done, it's done.

LISTFUL THINKING: USING LISTS TO BE MORE PRODUCTIVE, SUCCESSFUL AND LESS STRESSED

This book, published in 2014, and its companion, *Listful Living: A List-Making Journey To a Less Stressed You*, published in 2019, have been around a bit longer but the author Paula Rizzo has some nuggets of wisdom. Both discuss checklists, but from the perspective of checklists as productivity tools from home to work.

One topic of interest is mental fatigue. This quote from this book is from a psychotherapist and psychiatrist: "It takes mental work to keep things filed and stored and organized in your brain. And I think we underestimate how taxing it is to think." This discussion shows the use of checklists as memory tools. The question becomes: do you want to spend your "brain energy" trying to remember silly things like the next step in a process in a system that is not intuitive or the style for the second heading level in the document you're editing? Or do you want to let the checklist handle that, so you can use your "brain energy" to analyze data or to rewrite the text for a tough concept?

"AN ANALYSIS OF THE EFFECTIVENESS OF CHECKLISTS WHEN COMBINED WITH OTHER PROCESSES, METHODS AND TOOLS TO REDUCE RISK IN HIGH HAZARD ACTIVITIES"

This *Boeing Technical Journal* article by William Y. Higgins and Daniel J. Boorman is a thorough examination of the types of checklists, their use in different industries, and how critical prevention checklists are used to ensure that all tasks are carried out in high-hazard activities to improve safety, specifically at Boeing.

The introduction discusses the different types of checklists:
- ✓ Procedural: used in long, complex, or critical tasks that are performed only occasionally; these are "read and do" type checklists, where you read the items on the checklist, then do them sequentially.

- ✓ Preparation: used in multiple-step situations to ensure all items are performed.
- ✓ Problem-solving: used in complex procedures to discover sticking points, errors, or areas of difficulty through multiple-point questions.
- ✓ Prevention: critical checklists used to address errors in high-hazard areas that can result in injury, death, destruction, or negative impact.

While the article's focus is critical checklists for prevention, this book focuses on a comprehensive checklist that combines elements of the procedural and preparation checklists. But that doesn't mean there's nothing else to learn from the article. The article encourages users to develop checklists to fit unique challenges, and it acknowledges "expertise and experience as an essential foundation to the use of checklists."

This book asserts that comprehensive checklists should be created by the user and be based on their needs when performing the task. While it won't tell them how to edit or write or research, it will help with all the details before and after the task. If you don't have the expertise and experience, the checklist won't make you an editor or writer or other type of medical communicator. As the article notes, "checklists are only as good as the people using them."

BASIC VERSUS COMPREHENSIVE CHECKLISTS

Look for checklists on the internet, ask AI to create an editing checklist, or refer to your favorite medical writing textbook for an editing or writing checklist, and you're likely to find *basic* checklists. These basic checklists provide generic lists of things that need to be done, in no particular order, without style details, or process details, or time-tracking elements. They might provide a starting point, especially if you're a new medical communicator, but they are not specific enough to help you be efficient, consistent, and productive. If you want to grow as an editor or writer, you need to consider creating *comprehensive* checklists for your medical communication tasks. A *comprehensive* checklist for a specific task provides so much more than a *basic* checklist, as the figure on the next page shows:

COMPONENTS OF A COMPREHENSIVE CHECKLIST

PROCEDURAL CHECKLIST
Include the steps in the process, in the optimal order, including mechanics of systems

PREPARATION CHECKLIST
Include all the steps needed to ensure they are all performed

STYLE SHEET
Include style items specific to the client or type of work, punctuation standards, color schemes, abbreviations or specific terms used

TIME TRACKING
This can include anything helpful to track metrics for jobs, like start and stop times and details like length and difficulty

REMINDERS
These can be anything from "Perform Spell Check" to "Upload to database" to notes about specific client requirements

WHO SHOULD USE CHECKLISTS?

EVERYONE SHOULD USE CHECKLISTS!

If you're a newbie, developing checklists for yourself is a great way to learn and to improve your skills. They allow you to document your activities, experiment with your processes until you find the optimal flow, and track metrics for tasks. As a beginner, you might rely more on your checklists, and that's OK. Add what you need to your checklists as you learn and become a better medical editor or writer. The checklist is there for you: use it as needed to get things done and to learn your craft.

If you're experienced but not yet an expert, and you're not yet using checklists, you might be surprised by how using comprehensive checklists helps your workflow, assists in making sure you don't forget anything, and ensures that you complete your tasks with consistency.

For the experts already using checklists, consider adding elements of comprehensive checklists, such as reminders, steps in a process, or style items, that aren't in your current checklists. You'll find such additions helpful, and if you're in the position to be training or mentoring other editor or writers, you can share your checklists to give them a better start in their work.

Whether you're a newbie, an expert, or somewhere in between, you likely have too much to do in too little time. Being in this line of work means you have to value quality and consistency in the materials you edit and write, or you won't be successful. Creating and using comprehensive checklists will help you do your best and document all of it.

WHY SHOULD YOU USE CHECKLISTS?

Many people use checklists at home and at work for a variety of tasks. Why do you need to be convinced to create them for your work tasks? Given the time we spend at work and its importance to our lives, creating and using comprehensive checklists to make ourselves more efficient and consistent, increase productivity, and experience peace of mind should be an easy decision. There is some work involved, but the *How Do You Get Started?* chapter breaks it down into easy-to-follow steps.

As discussed in the *Basic Versus Comprehensive Checklists* chapter, what transforms a basic checklist into a comprehensive checklist are the following components: procedural checklist, preparation checklist, style sheet, time tracking, reminders. These additional components provide the benefits of memory, productivity, quality, and motivational tools:

MEMORY TOOL

Comprehensive checklists act as memory tools, capturing all of the details needed to accomplish a task in one place. Procedural steps, style details, and start and stop times can all be tracked in one place for a task.

✓ *Reduce cognitive load*

> Editing and writing tasks require so much human memory, details about systems, grammar and punctuation, style items, what to do first and last and in between. Putting as much of those details into your comprehensive checklist allows you to use your brain for solving new problems, finessing language and structure, and other more complicated issues. Not having to think ahead to the next step because you just have to follow the checklist is a relief!

✓ *Manage small details*

> When your comprehensive checklist acts as a style sheet, capturing relevant details about formatting, style, wording, and other details about a particular task in one place, it's infinitely more helpful. Especially for an editor, this ability to be consistent is invaluable, but it's helpful for many other types of tasks as well.
>
> Another way a checklist helps you manage small details is by allowing you to easily write notes about what's going on in a task. For example, is it exceptionally long? Not well structured? Is content hard to find for a topic? Tracking troublesome details allows you to look back later and remember the task.

✓ *Track metrics*

> Many people think they can estimate how long a task takes but most of us underestimate our time spent if we don't track it. Freelancers, in particular, could be losing money by underestimating the time it takes to complete a task. Though there are other ways to track your time on projects for invoices and metrics, tracking it on a checklist is a good start. It allows you to

track metrics (eg, how long a task takes, whoever was involved, and what type of work), and accurately estimate future projects.

 PAPER OR DIGITAL?

Paper checklists have some benefits: the physical act of checking something off of a paper checklist, a momentary break from staring at the screen, the ability to write small notes on paper.

But some people, especially if they have multiple monitors, or if they have everything else electronically, may want to use electronic checklists, and that's fine because there are so many options for electronic checklists. If you want to go in that direction, look into applications like Notion or Trello, or explore parts of the Microsoft Office Suite. OneNote has a great checklist function, and you can create checklists in Word, Excel, or even PowerPoint, complete with checkmarks!

PRODUCTIVITY TOOL

Comprehensive checklists act as productivity tools, showing the optimal order of steps to complete a task so you can get it done efficiently.

✓ *Increase efficiency*

   Going through the process of establishing what needs to be done, organizing steps within the task for optimal efficiency, and putting them into a comprehensive checklist allows you to follow a set list of items that you check off as you go. This approach makes you more efficient and more consistent in your editing, writing, and communication tasks.

✓ *Start and stop effectively*

   A comprehensive checklist keeps you on task, allowing you to stop and start back up with less loss of focus and certainly less worry. If and when you get interrupted, you'll know the last thing you did before you were interrupted. There's no need to backtrack and repeat multiple steps as you go through the task.

✓ *Induce flow*

   When you don't have to think about next steps, look up style items, or second guess yourself, you'll find yourself able to induce flow in your work, making you more productive and better able to handle higher level operations.

QUALITY TOOL

Comprehensive checklists act as a quality tool, ensuring you have essential information at your fingertips so you can be consistent in how you accomplish a task.

✓ **Increase consistency**
>With procedural steps, style details, and other information in your checklist, you can be sure to perform all the same steps the same way and in the same order, so you can be more consistent.

✓ **Reduce errors**
>Having details in front of you, being reminded of errors to watch out for, and working methodically through a task can reduce errors.

✓ **Document steps**
>Checking off steps as you go allows you to document the steps you've completed. And if deadlines or distractions prevent you from completing all the steps, that, too, will be documented in the checklist.

MOTIVATIONAL TOOL

A comprehensive checklist is a nice motivational tool, too.

✓ **See progress**
>Using a comprehensive checklist, you can see your progress as you go. And if you have good metrics, you'll be able to better estimate how much longer the task will take to complete by where you are in the checklist. And it often lets you know you're done. If you've ever worked on a project for too long, but you're worried whether you did enough, the checklist can let you know you did.

✓ *Recognize good work*

Adding a "Good Job!" section to the bottom of your comprehensive checklist gives you a chance to pat yourself on the back for a job well done. Find the product name spelled wrong? Good work! Find a math error in a table? Good work! Find a misspelling in a header? Good work!

BONUS

Why Should You Use Checklists? Why not? They're free. You don't need special software. You don't have to print them off if you don't have any paper or ink or a printer. The only cost is your time, but the return on investment is worth it.

HOW DO YOU GET STARTED?

How do you start creating a comprehensive checklist?

Here's the step-by-step process:

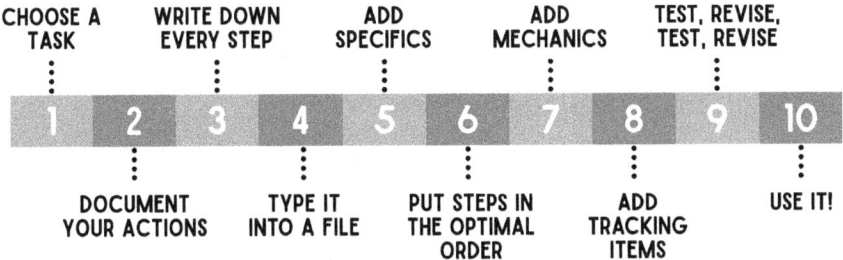

While it might seem like a lot of steps, some steps are simple, at least on the surface. And the hard ones? Doing the hard work in those steps is usually where you get the most benefit. For the right task, the benefits are more than worth the work.

1 CHOOSE A TASK

The first step is, of course, to choose a task. Tasks that are similar and repeated regularly are good candidates for a comprehensive checklist.

Consider the following scenario: You're working a full-time position as a medical editor editing five to 10 standard response letters every day. They're all similar in style and format, and even the content is similar in those in the same therapeutic area, so it can be really hard to remember what's been done to a particular document by the end of the day. Have the abbreviations been checked on this document or on the previous one?

Then consider that during your tenure you might access the documents in different systems and use different procedures, and those systems and procedures are frequently updated. You might be asked to start checking for new things or stop checking for other things. Documenting the steps in checklists would help you remember the latest process and requirements and perform the steps more efficiently without second-guessing yourself.

The checklist could also document current style and formatting details so that you can be sure you're up to date with the latest style guide, which is also perpetually evolving. Checking items off the checklist as you go enables you to start and stop an editing task without forgetting where you are, losing time duplicating your efforts as a result.

And with all of the different projects you have, tracking metrics for your tasks, whether you do it for yourself or because you must, is much easier if you do it on your checklists.

Types of tasks that need checklists:
- ✓ Tasks done often
- ✓ Processes with lots of details
- ✓ Processes with a lot of steps
- ✓ Tasks within systems that change frequently

✓ Documents with styles that change frequently
✓ Similar tasks that have small details that are different
✓ Tasks for which you want to track metrics

Sometimes infrequent tasks are good candidates for comprehensive checklists, too. How do you remember how to do something you do only twice a year if it has lots of steps, or the system you do it in is not intuitive? Such tasks are excellent candidates for a comprehensive checklist, especially if the process is not currently documented.

2 DOCUMENT YOUR ACTIONS

The second step is where you start doing the task, writing down everything you do. Just jot it down roughly, like brainstorming.

That can be difficult for folks, so here's some advice:
✓ Don't do this in a rush.
  Be patient and give yourself time to write down everything.
✓ Don't edit yourself.
✓ Don't assume anything.
  Have you ever gone on a really great vacation where you totally unplugged and didn't think about work? Maybe you came back with a clear head and tried to log in and couldn't remember your password. What if you went on one of those vacations and got back to your desk and your brain was empty? What would prompt you to remember what needs to be done? Write it down at that level.

✓ Don't skip steps now.

> If you decide you don't need them later, you can edit them out during testing. For now, just write it all down.

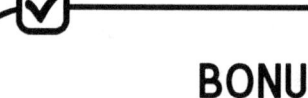

Going through this process of documenting your actions and writing down every step is also a good exercise for appreciating how much you do without thinking. Not just anyone can do what you do in the way that you do it!

3 WRITE DOWN EVERY STEP

The third step is an extension of the second step, but with the additional thought that you need to write down every step you take in performing a task.

Keep in mind that writing all of the steps down is where you get the productivity benefits of a checklist. Ever get interrupted in the middle of a task? If you did, and you had it marked on the checklist where you stopped, then you would know where to start back up again, without having to think about where you were and what you did.

Maybe you missed running a spell check or looking for abbreviations. The checkmarks in your checklist help you know what you have done and what still needs to be done.

Have you ever forgotten something because you thought you had already done it? Have you ever started doing something to a document, like checking the headings or finding an abbreviation that's often spelled wrong, then realized you already did this? Again, this is where the checklist helps you to not waste time duplicating efforts.

Are there items you're afraid you'll forget, or that you've forgotten when doing a task in the past? Write it down, so the checklist can help you get things done.

But keep in mind, this is not a "one and done." Sure, you can brainstorm what needs to be done for a particular task, but don't call that a comprehensive checklist. There's still work to be done.

4   TYPE IT INTO A FILE

The fourth step is where you take the steps from your handwritten notes to put it all together into a real document. You can use Word, Excel, or whatever makes sense for you. But don't edit it. Put it all in. You can take stuff out when you test it. And you should definitely test it.

When you create a format for it, don't forget a space for checkmarks!

5   ADD SPECIFICS

In the fifth step, you add specifics. Forget what you've seen on websites or in editing or writing textbooks. Those are basic checklists; you're a professional and need better tools.

For example, many checklists in textbooks or on websites are generic; they will say, *Check the headings*. When you're working with multiple clients for similar types of documents with different styles under a tight deadline, this isn't helpful.

Show what you want to see, say what it should be specifically. Don't just say, *Check the headings* on an editing checklist. *Show* how the headings should look:

Check/Modify Headings and Sections of Document	
Look for consistency in heading levels, order of sections, and use of bullets.	
Heading Level 1	SR Sections (*Ex:* Summary; Background; Clinical Data)
Heading Level 2	Topic or Name of Trial (*Ex:* Pharmacokinetics, The SAVOR Trial)
Heading Level 3	Study Citation. (*Ex:* Wallentin et al. *N Engl J Med.* 2009;361:1045-1057.)
Heading Level 4	Topic: (*Ex:* Objectives, Methods, Baseline Patient Characteristics, Results)
Heading Level 5	*Topic: (Ex: Design, Patients, Treatment Arms/Dosing, Primary Endpoint(s))*
Heading Level 6	Topic

Don't assume you'll remember what the headings should look like, all the steps in the process of the tasks, or the exact style items; write it all down.

6 PUTS STEPS IN THE OPTIMAL ORDER

This sixth step is where you reap many of the productivity benefits of a checklist, by thinking about how you can be more efficient in performing the task. What is the optimal order of steps? Working this out takes time, and you might have to test things a few different ways. Once you have it all typed into the checklist, it's easier to move things around.

If you're editing documents, for example, you want to group activities that require you to use the application's find function in one section. If you're editing or writing anything, you want to have spell check at the end.

You might still rearrange things in the test and revise step, but do your best based on what your instinct tells you at this time. Think about what makes sense for what needs to be done and put it in the checklist.

BONUS

 Sick of all the editing checklists? Even writers need to edit themselves from the draft versions to the final version. You can also use the elements of a good editing checklist to edit yourself when you're the writer.

Checklist Example

Here's an excerpt from an editing checklist that shows how I moved through editing a document in Word. I start by cleaning up spacing and formatting issues, because those are not usually tracked, and it gives me a nice clean document to work with, with no distractions.

The formatting checks are big-picture items that allow me to get a view of the whole document before I get down to the details in the body text. With short timelines, most editors no longer have the luxury of multiple passes with documents, so this sort of mini-pass gives them a snapshot of the document before they dive into it.

FORMATTING
Check Margins: 1" on top, bottom, left, and right
Check Footer: Left side should say: Section X.X or References or Abbreviations Right side should have auto-pagination: Page X of X
Check for Keep with Next near headings and tables
Check that spacing between paragraphs is consistent: spaces (¶) or consistent spacing before and after (3pt/6 pt).
Check Bulleted and Numbered Lists Make sure bullets and numbers begin at the left margin and that the tab is only .25 for each level.
Check Size of Font • Body Text: 10 pt Times New Roman • Headings: 12 pt Times New Roman
Check Justification • Check that body text, bullets, and references are left justified.
Check Spacing • Do a Find for period followed by 2 spaces; replace with period followed by 1 space. • Do a Find for 2 spaces; replace with 1 space..
Check Headings and Sections of Document: Look for consistency in heading levels, order of sections, and use of bullets.
2.2 HEADING LEVEL 1: Bold, Small Caps 2.2.1 HEADING LEVEL 2: Roman, Small Caps 2.2.1.1 Heading Level 3: Roman, Initial Caps (no number) Heading Level 4: Underlined, Initial Caps (no number) *Heading Level 5*: Italics, Initial Caps (no number) Heading Level 6: Roman, Initial Caps

7 ADD MECHANICS

In the seventh step, you put the specifics of processes, what you might have to do in particular systems. This is especially important if your systems or processes have recently changed, if they are not intuitive, or if they are so complicated you need to refer to instructions. In those cases, put the instructions in the checklist. Someday in the future, you might take them back out, but if you need them now, put them in. This checklist is for you to use as you see fit. It should grow and change as you do. This is a judgement-free zone; if you need reminders and instructions, add them.

If you save to a shared drive, you might not need this level of detail about your systems, but if you use a document management system (eg, Veeva Vault), a content management system (CMS), or a component content management system (cCMS), this could be helpful.

If a task is something you just know how to do, then you can write, simply, "perform spell check." And even if you know you need to perform the spell check, this is one of those things you can't afford to forget to do, so it needs to go on the checklist.

Checklist Example

Here's an excerpt from a checklist showing the last few steps of editing a standard response document (see the full checklist in the *Checklist Examples* chapter). These steps are the mechanics that need to be done to complete a task in the systems I worked in. We all need to run a spell check on our documents; it also covers things like making sure the cross-references are updated, checking the document one last time (if you've tracked changes, for example, checking it with and without those changes displayed), saving it, and some of the tasks we need to do once we put the document in the system.

FINAL TOUCHES
Run Spell Check
Update Fields for Cross-references Attempt to correct any "Bookmark not Defined" errors; if it's too complicated, ask author to correct.
Change View to 100% and Look Over SR One More Time • Make sure tables break cleanly over pages and that column headings are repeated, as necessary. • Replace hyphens and spaces in bad line breaks with nonbreaking hyphens or spaces.
Save Document
CHECK DOCUMENT BACK IN Indicate what was done to the SR in the Description box. (*Ex:* Edited SR. Minor changes. OR Standard edit/tracked changes.)
Check Rendition in Viewer • Open in Full Screen. • Look for endnotes and cross-references coming in at a different size than the rest of the text or cross-references coming in not superscripted. • Fix any issues, then re-upload a new version and repeat this step.

8 ADD TRACKING ITEMS

In the eighth step, add tracking items. Maybe you don't think you need this, but you'll be better off tracking something now and finding out you don't need it later or that it is nice to have, than to not track it and wish you had.

This section can be anything you need it to be. Does your boss want to know how much time you spend on a particular task? Do you need to prove that something that seems easy is actually more complicated and time-consuming than it looks? For editing tasks, are there certain authors, teams, or topics that take more time, either because the work comes to you in a worse state or because it is just more complicated? These conditions can be tracked in checklists and summarized into reports or informal discussions with others.

Paper checklists are also a useful tool for remembering what was going on with a particular task if you're asked about it later. And if you didn't have time to check or do everything in your checklist, you'll have a note of it and your tracking information might show why. For example, your tracking section could note whether the document was a rush or the number of pages (which shows if it's a long or short document), which might explain not completing all of the elements of the edit.

You can also use the checklist to track details specific to a task in case things crop up that were not on the checklist. This might happen when you're working with new products or subject matter. You might have common terms in the checklist and many more in the style guide. But with a new product or subject matter, you might find yourself looking up new terms in a medical dictionary, or consulting other documents or with other writers for more information or to learn the proper way to use a word. Documenting these details on the checklist enables you to be consistent in terminology in future projects.

Checklist Examples

The time-tracking section can look different from task to task.

In this excerpt from a freelance project, I edited one-page documents two or three times a month, then invoiced after completing a set number of them. The sheet contains three of these, and it helps me quickly see how long they have each taken me instead of assuming. And when I have more than one of them in progress, it reminds me to do all of the steps to each of them.

Client:								
Time: ___	___	___	Time: ___	___	___	Time: ___	___	___
START	STOP	SPENT	START	STOP	SPENT	START	STOP	SPENT
Run Spell Check								
Clean up author section								
• Ensure consistent names, titles, and locations								
Edit titles								
Edit main text								
Run Spell Check								
Save Document								
Email back to Client								

The excerpt on the next page shows tracking items in an editing checklist I used. You can be specific and spell out whatever details are helpful to you. If you are an editor supporting a whole team of writers (listed as Owners in this example), and you need to tell your boss who has been sending you work and who has not, a quick flip through the checklists will show you that certain writers or certain teams are sending you work. Later, you can consolidate the items manually. I consolidated the information monthly to get a better idea of what I was working on.

```
Owner: _____    Product: _____    Editor: _____
Date Received: _____    Date Due: _____    Rush: Yes  No    SR#: _____
Approve/Activate: Yes  No    Track Changes: Yes  No    # of Pages: _____
Time: ___  ___  ___    Date Completed: _____    Entered in Tracker: _____
      START STOP SPENT
```

9 TEST, REVISE, TEST, REVISE

This last step is where you figure out what really works and what doesn't. Sometimes you might create a checklist that you do not ultimately need, but you're much more likely to have the opposite effect of wondering how in the world you ever did without your checklist.

In this sequence of steps, you want to test the checklist with a real task and edit it as you go. When you're done with the task, update the checklist, print it out and test it again. You're not stuck with your original sequence of steps. Try something new if the steps don't seem to be flowing. Test it, update it, then test it again.

10 USE IT!

The last step is the most important: use your checklist! Using it repeatedly to be more efficient and consistent will make all of the work worth your time and effort.

CASE STUDY: MANUSCRIPT EDITING CHECKLIST

As you think about how to make your own comprehensive checklists, it's helpful to see how someone else creates and uses a comprehensive checklist for a common medical communication task. As an editor, I use a manuscript editing checklist because the checklist keeps me on task, reminds me of the many details I need to check and track, makes me a better and faster editor, and allows me to track metrics and accurately estimate future projects. Every manuscript is different, and every journal is different, so it can be easy to get tripped up by the differences and miss something. My checklist makes sure I do everything I intend to do when editing a manuscript.

The next few pages dive a little deeper into my checklist for editing manuscripts for a medical journal to show how you might put together a comprehensive checklist for a task you do.

As an added bonus for folks new to manuscript editing, walking through my manuscript editing checklist allows you see into the process of editing manuscripts, formatting them, and submitting them to journals. Some assumptions in regard to this generic checklist are that it will be printed out, and that you'll be editing, formatting, and submitting a manuscript to a medical journal.

TRACKING SECTION

```
Client: _____    Project # _____    Additional Contact: _____
Manuscript (long title): _____
_____
Manuscript (short title): _____
Journal (name): _____    Journal (abbreviation): _____
Instructions to Authors site: _____
Date Due: _____  Pages: _____  Refs: _____  Figures: _____  Tables: _____
Time: ____  ____  ____   Time: ____  ____  ____   Time: ____  ____  ____
     START  STOP  SPENT        START  STOP  SPENT        START  STOP  SPENT
Time: ____  ____  ____   Time: ____  ____  ____   Time: ____  ____  ____
     START  STOP  SPENT        START  STOP  SPENT        START  STOP  SPENT
```

The top of my manuscript editing checklist always contains essential information about the project. Most journals require a long title (what's published) and a short title (or running title, which may be used as a header). You have to know the journal and where they keep the instructions to authors if you'll be formatting and submitting the manuscript. Having the journal abbreviation allows you to use it in email subject lines and the file folder and file name.

Having the due date on the checklist can help you keep track of the project. Documenting the number of pages allows you to track projects, so you can look back at the checklists in the future to gauge future project metrics (how long it took vs how long the document was).

As a freelancer, it's good to track hours, whether you're billing hourly or by the project, so you know if you're accurately estimating your quotes. Creating multiple spaces for timing is helpful if you tend to jump in and out of projects.

FIRST PASS SECTION

	Run PerfectIt
	Edit title page Ensure it has everything required from journal
	Clean up author section • Ensure consistent names, titles, affiliations, and locations • Ensure there is contact information for lead or corresponding author on cover page • Ensure there is contact information for all authors (if needed for submission)
	Edit abstract Make sure it has the following sections (or similar as required by journal): • Background • Methods • Results • Conclusion
	Count number of words and compare to journal requirements: Journal Req: Abstract:
	Count number of keywords and compare to journal requirements: Journal Req: Main text:
	Edit keywords

In the first pass, it's helpful to begin with a run-through of PerfectIt to clear out some inconsistencies, get a feel for the abbreviations being used, and start with a cleaner document. Another assumption is that the editing is being done in Word, using tracked changes for content changes, but often accepting or not tracking formatting changes.

The first page of the manuscript is often the title page, and most author instructions are specific about how they want the author information to look and what's needed, like author names, affiliations, and locations. This section just ensures that you check that the author information on the title page meets the requirements of the journal.

The next page of the manuscript (or immediately following the title page) is often the abstract, which might be structured (like what's shown on the checklist) or unstructured, meaning it runs as a paragraph. If it's structured, the journal might require that the sections include specific headings and information, which might or might not match what's shown on the checklist. If the abstract format isn't specified, this information can be added for the author as a starting point.

Almost all journals have a word limit for abstracts, typically 250 to 300 words. It's sometimes helpful to quickly read it on first pass, then come back to the abstract again later to make sure it reflects the rest of the manuscript, and to trim it if it's too long.

Journals often require keywords to be included, usually three to six terms you think will help people find your article on the internet. If the manuscript doesn't have keywords, but the journal requires them, you can add the section and some keywords for the authors, in tracked changes, so they know to check them. It's helpful to have a spot on the checklist to either edit what they have or add something to the manuscript.

MAIN TEXT SECTION

Edit main text	
Make sure it has the following sections:	
• Introduction	
• Methodology	
• Results and Discussion (consider whether strict separation of these sections is important)	
• Conclusion	
Count number of words and compare to journal requirements:	
Journal Req:	Main text:
Count number of figures and compare to journal requirements:	
Journal Req:	Manuscript:
Ensure figures are the right format and size	
Count number of tables and compare to journal requirements:	
Journal Req:	Manuscript:
Ensure tables follow journal requirements	

The checklist doesn't tell you how to edit the main text of the manuscript; it shows you all the areas that you need to edit to ensure you don't forget any as you hop around checking various elements. You can certainly add anything you need to the checklist to assist you in editing a manuscript: other reminders based on things you tend to miss, or things you see that the authors you work with obviously struggle with. If you're concerned about not knowing what to look for when editing manuscripts, get a copy of *Editing Scientific and Medical Research Articles* by Claire Bacon (see the *References* chapter).

The next sections have checks for the number of words in the manuscript versus the journal requirements, the number of figures versus the journal requirements, confirming that figures are the right format and size, the number of tables versus journal requirements, and confirming that tables are the right format.

Journals often have specific requirements for the format of the figures and tables, so you need to check them against the journal's requirements. Similarly, journals are often particular about how figures should be provided to them. When formatting the manuscript and submitting to the journal, these checks are an essential part of this task. Likewise, there are often restrictions around how many figures and tables the authors can provide in the main article, so you might need to count the numbers of table and figures and compare against the journal requirements.

ABBREVIATIONS SECTION

	Check/Fix Abbreviations and Acronyms • Ensure that the composite words of abbreviations and acronyms are spelled out on first use in body text, followed by the abbreviation and/or acronym in parentheses. *Headings should have full version in most cases.*
	• Use abbreviations and acronyms only if the term is used ≥3 times in the document. Note: If using Find and Replace to help locate abbreviations and acronyms, look for both the spelled-out versions and the abbreviations. • Make sure that abbreviations and acronyms are used consistently within the manuscript.

Next up are some reminders to check the abbreviations used. Some of this can be done or helped with PerfectIt, but there's often still work to do with this section. The rules cited here are from the *AMA Manual of Style* (AMA) (see the *References* chapter), but of course, change your checklist if you have another house style, other style guides to follow, or the journal instructions are different.

REFERENCES SECTION

	Edit references • Look up each reference and correct if needed • Edit according to journal's author instructions and *AMA Manual of Style*
	Edit supplementary materials
	Edit conflict of interest statements / funding statements / disclosures
	Edit CRediT author statement
	Edit Acknowledgements Make sure you are acknowledged as appropriate

The references section is usually at the end of the manuscript, so you could handle them after you have edited the main text, though some folks prefer to start their editing task with checking the references. The references can be a challenging section to edit, so this is a good reminder to look them up and make sure they follow AMA or the journal's requirements, if different from AMA.

The supplementary materials can be extensive, so they get a place on the checklist, even though there might not be any, or they might not be provided, depending on the article and the client.

The requirements for conflicts of interest can vary widely from journal to journal. Many require a statement at the end of the document but others require it on the title page, then they also require a separate PDF to be signed and submitted for each author. Your authors may say they have no conflicts of interest, but you may need to dive a little deeper because the journal's submission process might ask specific questions or ask for more information.

If the journal requires the Contributor Roles Taxonomy (CRediT) author statement, you'll need to make sure it's included, and so it has a space on my checklist. In case your authors don't know about it, check out the CRediT author statement format (see the *References* chapter) so you can educate them if needed. Even if the journal does not require that specific CRediT author statement, the journal might require some sort of author statement. If the instructions for authors specify what the statements should say, follow those instructions. If there's no format listed and there's no author statement in the manuscript, the CRediT format is a safe bet for fulfilling the requirement.

The Acknowledgment section is often at the end of the manuscript, but some journals require it and/or the conflicts of interest on the title page. Be sure there's a section if it's required, and whether you're an editor or writer, ensure you're acknowledged for your contributions. For example, it could say, "We thank Kelly Schrank, MA, ELS, of Bookworm Editing Services LLC for her editorial services in preparing the manuscript for publication."

AUTHOR INSTRUCTIONS SECTION

Notes from Journal's Author Instructions	
Additional materials needed	

Depending on how extensive the author instructions are, how you save and use them, and how much their style differs from what's already in the manuscript, this section might not be used, or there might be a lot of notes. You can include it or not, based on how you like to work and how much you think you'll use it.

THE FINAL TOUCHES SECTION

FINAL TOUCHES
Run spell check
Run PerfectIt
Turn off track changes
Change View to 100% <ul><li>Look over one more time in **All Markup**</li><li>Reread comments to ensure they are still needed and worded appropriately</li><li>Look over one more time in **No Markup**</li></ul>
Save Document
Email back to author in email subject line that matches naming convention

The final touches section includes a reminder to run a spell check and another round of PerfectIt, and to look it over again from a high level, preferably in both All Markup and No Markup. This is a good time to read through all of the comments to make sure that questions were not answered later in the reading, and to go through the language again to ensure it's respectful and helpful to the author(s).

WHEN READY TO SUBMIT SECTION

WHEN READY TO SUBMIT
Edit cover letter
Ensure that author order and affiliations in system matches manuscript
Ask authors to provide any conflicts of interest statements / funding statements / disclosures
Ask if they have suggested reviewers or not-suggested reviewers (if provided in submission system)
Confirm manuscript type
Ensure you have all of the appropriate files to upload • Ensure cover letter and manuscript are together or separate as indicated in journal instructions • Ensure figures are separate files (or not) as required

The last section is for those who submit manuscripts to journals on behalf of authors. Depending on the process with that client, you might or might not handle some or all of this. If you never handle this for your clients, you don't need to include this section in your checklists. If you sometimes do this type of work, you can include this section in your checklists, but put an X there instead of a checkmark when working for a client where you don't do this work.

HOW DO YOU KNOW YOU HAVE GOOD CHECKLISTS?

So how do you know you have good checklists?

✓ When you start a new type of project, and you feel lost without a checklist

If you are an experienced professional, you know what to do when you get a project. But as an experienced professional, who is good at what you do, you may also end up with a lot of projects. If you find yourself with many different types of projects, with different clients, on different systems, having comprehensive checklists for the many tasks you work on may help you keep them all straight and know where you are with any of them at any one time. As a newbie, learning new things all the time, how do you keep track of it all? A comprehensive checklist can be a great tool for solidifying your skills and knowledge into a system that helps you do a better job every day.

✓ When you find an error your editing checklist told you to look for

Has this ever happened to you? You get caught up in a messy document and there is so much to fix that you forget to check something. Sometimes, it's something small, but other times, it's important, like misspelling the product name or headings that end up with typos. When you look back at the checklist, and it tells you to check for something, like consistent capitalization in headings, or that abbreviations are spelled out on first use, and then you do the check and find the error or inconsistency the checklist told you to look for, it's a relief!

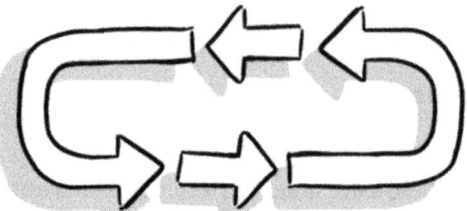

✓ When you have peace of mind when working on something

When you work on a task with a comprehensive checklist, you can pick up where you left off with confidence despite interruptions, distractions, or an "off day." You feel better knowing you did what you set out to do with that task. That peace of mind can make a big difference in your productivity.

✓ **When you are asked for metrics, and you can confidently give an estimate because you have the data in your checklists**

Whether doing freelance work, or working in a full-time position, metrics are important. Clients want to know, *How much is this going to cost me?* Co-workers or manager want to know, *How long will it take you to do this?* You can track metrics in apps, but tracking your metrics in checklists for a task is also an option.

✓ **When you go back and re-read your comments to the authors because the editing checklist reminded you to do it**

Can you be little snarky in your initial run-through of a document? Some editors admit to making quick notes that might be a little snarky on the first pass. But it is essential to read through the comments again to make sure they are professional and helpful, that they are still relevant and important, and that items questioned have not been answered now after reading through the rest of the manuscript.

✓ When you are confident you have completed a project because you have checked everything off on your checklist

Have you ever had a project or document drag on until you were sick of it? You just want it off your plate, but how do you know if you have done enough? Sometimes a checklist can help you know you have done enough and that it is time to move it off your plate.

INTERVIEWS WITH CHECKLIST ENTHUSIASTS

This section provides an exploration into how other medical communicators use checklists.

INTERVIEW WITH A CONTINUING MEDICAL EDUCATION (CME) WRITER AND CHECKLIST ENTHUSIAST

ALEXANDRA HOWSON PHD, CHCP, E-RYT
WRITE MEDICINE
AUTHOR OF *WRITECME ROADMAP*
HOST OF THE WRITE MEDICINE PODCAST
HTTPS://WWW.ALEXHOWSON.COM/

How did you get started using checklists in your work?

I was always making to-do lists as a kid, as a teenager. There's something very calming about having written down all the kinds of tasks that you have to do.

And then I was a trauma OR [operating room] nurse for many years. And this was before the World Health Organization's Surgical Safety Checklist, which I think came into being in 2009. When I was working in trauma ORs in the 1980s and the early 1990s we didn't have formal checklists, but we definitely had a checklist mentality for everything that you do in the OR. There is a series of steps in a particular order that you have to take, and so I think that just kind of spilled over when I was an academic after I was a trauma OR nurse.

And then for the last 20 years, I've been an independent CME writer. And so it just seemed like the logical thing to do at the start of every project: create a checklist. And some of those checklists or checklist elements are tasks, and some of them are process steps.

Okay, new project, new checklist. So that's how I got started.

Why do you use checklists?

I don't want to forget things. And I know that I do forget things. And sometimes with newish tasks, they've got extra steps or extra tasks that might not have been part of previous projects that I've done, so I want to make sure that I don't forget that.

It's a methodical way to make sure that I don't miss any vital information or steps in the process. I'm not leaving it all to chance. I'm not leaving it all to memory. If it's project-based work, it's a good way to know that you're doing everything that you said that you would do for the client.

When I'm estimating projects, I am listing out all the tasks that a project is going to take in order to execute it. Maybe not on the actual proposal itself, but certainly for myself. And so that just becomes the checklist. But then when I get all of the briefing material before, as we're kicking off, I'm adding in new things to the checklist. It gives me a picture of what it's going to take to execute any particular project.

How many checklists do you think you have?

Every project that I've ever done in the last 20 years, more or less, has a checklist. So we're talking about hundreds of projects.

Some of those projects and some of those checklists are pretty similar, but most of them are unique, because they're unique to that project.

I was just having a conversation with a coaching client about standing operating procedures [SOPs]. I run a professional development program for medical writers who are specializing in CME. And I was thinking that one of the things that I should probably do is create checklists for different types of projects, like slide decks, assessments, etc. I actually have one for needs assessments. But generic checklists that people can use as a starter pack. Here are all the steps you really need to be thinking about. You can add your own, you can customize, because that would be a kind of helpful visual. So a checklist is just a no brainer for me, for any project.

I have an extensive checklist for podcast production as well.

What is your process for putting together a new checklist?

So if it's a project, then I'm already starting the checklist process when I'm estimating; I'm trying to figure out what all the tasks are for a given project. Then if the project is given the green light, I have that as the foundation for building the process checklist. And at that point, I'm usually subcategorizing and subdividing tasks into even smaller tasks or steps.

So I think that's typically how I would do it.

I'm not always good at then retrospectively building the next checklist based on the last checklist as I really should be because everything is moving so fast. But a retrospective is a really good way to make sure that you covered all your bases and you can add in that new information that emerged in the process of doing the project. And that's good, not just for the sake of having a complete checklist, but it's good because the next time you come to estimate that type of project, you have that information and you can build that in the next checklist on an as-needed basis. You know this happened the last time, you should really make sure that you have a contingency plan for that.

That totally makes sense that where you might start offering things you didn't think to offer before, because you did something with somebody and you're like, *Okay, let's put this in at the beginning of the process, make sure they want to add it to the cost,* **and just making sure everything is documented.**

I think that's another function of a checklist. It becomes a source of documentation about what you've done and it feeds into your future estimation and then you can look at checklists for similar projects over time and see what's changed. And use that to think about your estimation process, your budgeting, service offerings, all those things. So it becomes a resource for your business if you're freelance.

Would you consider your checklists basic or comprehensive? How would you differentiate between the two?

I've never thought about them in those ways. My podcast checklist is pretty comprehensive. It has several different categories, and then sub-tasks or sub-steps within each category. For some projects that are quick turnaround, where you've done it so many times, then that would definitely be a sort of basic checklist and it might even be a mental checklist.

But I don't really make the differentiation. I know that I work better when I have a checklist than when I don't. I think for all of us when we're working on projects that we know very well how to execute, we've done many of them, and we've done them many times, then we are working in intuitive mode. I think a checklist introduces reflection, and when you start to reflect, then you can slow down. I do think there's a braking function with a checklist.

I'm trying to think about the difference between a basic checklist on a website for a task versus a comprehensive checklist, like your podcast checklist that's got procedure, style, everything you need in one place.

I think that's a really great point. And I do think that there's two things. One is that the business of having everything in one place is important as my business has grown over the years and as it has also grown in different directions. Especially where I have pivoted my business, I'm very conscious I'm using way more tools and software programs than I did a decade ago or even five years ago. I've got Google, ClickUp, Notion; I use a ton of different software platforms. And so having a checklist is a way of bringing all those different threads together. And for any one project, it's not just the tasks and the steps. There are different strands to any one project as well and different databases or different literature that you're looking at, different types of materials. And I don't think I am naturally methodical, so the checklist really helps kind of rein all of that in and just prevents that sense of rising panic in what could be an overwhelming project.

Yeah, I agree with that completely. I think the other thing you were saying about getting a checklist from a website as being basic. I think that's probably true, but I also think it's also really helpful. If you have a kind of starting checklist and because it prompts you to think about this thing over here. I can add this to the checklist and you can build it from something that somebody else has already started to put together.

What do you consider the benefits of using checklists in your work?

It gives me a visual guide, and it provides parameters or guardrails. Actually, it's, *this is all I need to do. If I stick to this, I'll be good* and so it helps to reduce that sense of overwhelm at the beginning of a project. It helps to create a path: *Oh, this is where I need to go.* I can see the end point. I like to be able to check things off. Sometimes it's really nice just to be like, *You know what? The checklist says I'm done.* And so, it's those things. It's also a kind of methodical way of making sure that you cover everything and don't leave things to chance. So the main benefit is that it's just reassuring that I'm doing all the things that I thought at the beginning of this project, I would have to do in order to get it done. It doesn't mean that every checklist is perfect.

How do you know you have a good checklist?

Yeah, that's a good question. I'm not sure that's a question I have asked myself. I mean, for me, a good checklist is a checklist I can get through and I know the project is done and the client likes it. Or the podcast episode is out. Success. What I thought I was going to do is done. That's a good checklist.

Would you say you're a checklist user, a checklist fan, a checklist enthusiast, or a checklist specialist?

I'm definitely an enthusiast. For me, it's an essential tool. And it's a really basic thing that you can do for yourself just to bring a little bit of ease and steadiness into your work. You've got your checklist, and it's telling you what you need to do.

I'm thinking about this: you're obviously experienced, and you still find value in checklists; how do you think it's different for those who are new or even those who are intermediate level?

In terms of developing checklists and using checklists, I think the challenge when you're new is, you know, you don't know what you don't know. And so, if you're doing a new type of project, then you're starting from scratch. You're starting from not really having a clear sense of what all the steps and what all the tasks might actually be for that project. But over time, it's an iterative process. I think that's the difference. And then once you've done something a few times, then you've got a pretty solid idea of what needs to be in that checklist. Yeah, you can add to it. As I say, every project is different. There's some plug-and-play elements, but there are some new pieces as well. So I think the main thing when you're new is, start from where you are.

Engage with your network, ask some questions, ask your client tons of questions so that you can pull all of this into your checklist. Don't be afraid to ask those questions because that will help you really build a robust task or process checklist. And then over time, you know it kind of becomes second nature. *OK, I've gotta build my checklist; here's what the client needs. Here's what I know here. Here are some gaps and what I know I have to ask those questions to make sure I get the information from the client.* And you sort of build your checklist that way.

What advice do you have for others when it comes to creating and using checklists?

If you're starting a new project, then write down every task or step in the process that you think you are going to need to do. Second, reflect on gaps in your information or your knowledge. And third, seek out answers to those gaps. Ask your client for more information. Ask your network to give you some ideas about what you might be missing. And then organize your checklist. I mean, you can organize checklists in lots of different ways by subcategory, by type of task, by process step. You know, play around with that to see what works for you. And you know, if all else fails, just start with a numbered list from one to 175. And play around with that and see what works.

INTERVIEW WITH A MANUSCRIPT EDITOR AND CHECKLIST ENTHUSIAST

CRYSTAL HERRON
REDWOOD INK
WWW.REDWOODINK.COM

How did you get started using checklists in your work?

I attended a talk that you gave at an AMWA conference! I had always liked "to do" lists, and I was intrigued by the topic of your talk. So I went, and I became an instant fan.

Why do you use checklists?

Before I went to your talk, there were times when I would forget to do something when I was editing. I would try to just have it all in my head. And then I kept noticing that I'd send a project back to a client and think, *Shoot, I forgot to do this thing*. And so I started putting tasks in a checklist. But not just a checklist of things to do. In your presentation at AMWA, I loved that you talked about organizing tasks into categories, and in the order that you're going to do them, so I started to do that. Then my checklists helped me make sure that I didn't miss anything, made the process more efficient, and even helped me track editing nuances so I didn't have to look them up over and over again. Now I have checklists for everything. Checklists also helped me think about editing more systematically because everything tends to be intertwined. So that was also really helpful.

How long has it been then since you've been using them like this?

Since my first AMWA conference in 2019.

I try to differentiate the kind of checklist that I talk about as being *comprehensive*, but I never really thought of what to call other people's checklists that aren't like mine. And so I thought maybe they're *basic*. What do you think about my terminology, basic or comprehensive, does that make sense to you?

It does. I think that distinction is important, because it's not just a checklist of things you need to do. There's a structure and a system to it. And I also know that a checklist that I might use isn't necessarily going to be good for someone else. I've had coaching clients ask if they can have a copy of my checklist, and my response is that they can, but they will have different needs and will need to customize it for themselves.

But I like *comprehensive*. The only thing I wonder is if you want to also capture that the idea of systematic, methodical, ordered, or something like that as well because that aspect has also been really helpful.

Any other thoughts on how to differentiate between the two?

I like having a basic checklist and then building on to it to make it comprehensive. I remember going to your checklist session and thinking, *Oh, it's a checklist, maybe it'll be a* little bit *helpful*. And then when I saw what was possible, I thought, *Oh, I have not actually thought about the potential of checklists.* So I think *comprehensive* helps to make sure that people know it's not just their to-do list of checkmarks. There's also a strategy behind it that's really helpful.

How many checklists would you say you have in your work?

A lot. I have checklists related to each type of work I do. I have checklists for editing, speaking, and creating YouTube videos. With editing, I have a lot of checklists because I have them by manuscript and document type. I also have them by style guide type because I primarily work in AMA style, and only sometimes APA style [*Publication Manual of the American Psychological Association*], and there are certain things that I tend to overlook in APA style, so I have a special checklist. I also have checklists for different types of grants. And then I also have client-specific checklists, especially for a journal that I work with because they have their own set of guidelines. So I also have a checklist for each of the article types that that journal has. A lot of the tasks are similar and have a similar structure. So I started with a checklist from one type of manuscript and then created variations for other manuscript types rather than building them all from scratch.

So when you say you have the style guide, the type of work, and the client, do you end up putting it into one for that client for a manuscript with AMA? Or are you following three checklists? Do you know what I'm saying?

Oh, yes. So I have specific checklists for a manuscript in AMA style, or a case report in AMA style, or a manuscript in APA style. And then for the journal I work with, I have more specific checklists that include the journal name and the type of article. For the client, I also return a cover sheet with the project. These cover sheets are also specific to the project and capture some checklist items that I think are important to share with clients, such as common stylistic changes or word limits required by the agency. I probably have twenty to thirty checklists. It might sound like a lot, but the more specific they are to the project, the more helpful they are.

How do you use them?

I always print them out. There's a sense of satisfaction I get by checking items off with a pen. But I also have a built-in notes section so that if there's something that comes up as I'm working on the document, I can make note of anything else that I might need to check that isn't already on my checklist. Also, as I'm editing, I add a lot of comments to the document to explain my rationale for making changes, and sometimes they can be redundant. So I also have a section on the checklist to track the snippets or comments I make so that I don't repeat a long comment over and over again and burden the author with more comments than are really necessary. So I customize my checklists and build in features that help me with my process. And I like to print them out to make all those notes.

Also, I've organized the tasks in the order I edit a document. I start off with quicker "do it and check it" items like running PerfectIt or fixing the formatting. And then I read and edit the document, so the checks don't happen as quickly. Then at the end, I go back through the checklist to ensure I've checked everything off.

So if you have a new checklist, what's your process for getting that put together?

Well, my first inclination is to try to automate it. So I go back to one of my previous checklists and find the one that is most similar to the checklist I want to create. And then I update that version based on what I think is going to need to be included for this document. Then I print it out to test it. As I work through the document, I make comments on things I should add or take out. And then I'll update it. I often need to repeat this testing and refining process a couple of times to "finalize" the checklist, although I continue to make changes to the checklist as I need to.

So for something that's brand new, like your YouTube videos, how did you do that?

YouTube is new for me, so I had to create a brand new checklist rather than simply modify an old one. So I took my template style and noted all the challenges I had and all the mistakes I made while making the first video, so I didn't repeat them.

Then I categorized smaller tasks into larger tasks I needed to do, like planning the script, recording the video, editing the video, posting the video, etc. So I reviewed my list and figured out how to chunk the tasks into categories. Then I looked at the order of the tasks to put them in the most efficient order. And then I moved into the testing and refining phase. So for the next video, I used it and noted what needed to be tweaked. And I did that with a handful of videos until I got to a place I'm happy with.

I think that's also one reason I update my checklists every year in my checklist of things to do in January. I think that regularly updating checklists is important, because if something changes, you need to change the checklist. Or if you notice that you tend to make a certain error, or you no longer need to include a certain task that you've mastered, you need to change the checklist to optimize it for your needs now rather than what your needs were in the past. And this practice helps you stay current and recognize how you've grown in your work.

I like to talk about how you don't realize how much you do sometimes until you put it on a checklist. There's a lot of things you check, and there's PerfectIt, and there's spell check, and there's all these finds and replaces and there's a lot of stuff that we do. And it really helps to be able to document that and to be able to say, *Oh my gosh, no wonder this takes so long.*

So that's interesting. I hadn't thought about it from that lens. Also, sometimes as an editor, it can be challenging to prove your value. How much you do; why does this take so long?

But I think a checklist can be a great way to show your value and raise awareness of all the things that you do. For example, I have a four-page checklist for a proposal, and I anticipate that if a client saw that, they'd realize that editing isn't just reading and giving some superficial feedback. There is a lot that goes into it.

So what would you consider the benefits of using them in your work?

Checklists help me follow a systematic process with a strategy. They also help with consistency either between team members or just across the documents that you're working on.

I also find them helpful for tracking changes in style guidelines. For example, if there's a sudden change in AMA style, and I want to make sure that I pay attention to it, I'll add it to my checklist. That way I don't overlook it or have to look it up again.

Creating checklists also helps you really think about what you're doing and why you're doing it that way. And when you keep updating the checklist, you have those opportunities to optimize what you're doing, especially in the beginning.

How do you know you have good checklists?

Of course, there's the whole idea that you don't miss anything and you don't make a mistake. But it's also when you don't want to work without a checklist. I think that's when you know you have a good tool.

So what is your level of commitment to checklists: checklist user, checklist fan, checklist enthusiast, or checklist specialist?

I am definitely a checklist enthusiast. I don't know that I could call myself a specialist. I probably wouldn't say specialist because I haven't read the books, done the research, and that kind of thing. So I'm probably like at the very high end of enthusiast.

So what advice do you have for others when it comes to creating and using checklists?

Take one of your trainings.

And I'll also give some general advice that I give to people whenever they're using something new or trying something new: do it more than once because the first time that you do it, you're going to feel uncomfortable and may hit a few speedbumps. So try it at least twice. And know that checklists are for *you* and they're flexible. You can adapt them so that they best suit what you need.

INTERVIEW WITH A REGULATORY WRITER AND CHECKLIST SPECIALIST

CHRIS FAISON
FAISON ASSOCIATES
WWW.FAISONASSOCIATES.COM

How did you get started using checklists for your work?

Pretty simply by having them as required elements for in-house positions. This is part of the SOP, or a part of a work instruction, and it's mandatory. Here's your checklist. And you need to sign off saying that you actually did check off all these things. So it's a responsibility of the job whether it's in-house clinical operations where I started or in medical writing. I find that they're even more widely used in medical writing than in clinical operations. Everyone uses the same one, for consistency, and they are provided by the company. Usually there is a checklist specific to a document type. There is an investigator's brochure checklist detailing what you need to cover. And there are clinical study reports [CSR] protocol, and protocol amendment checklists. Each document type is going to have its own checklist. So that's how I started using them.

Why do you use checklists?

Oh, I have an interesting case study as far as that goes. I hired a team of medical writers to work on a client's project. It was one of those situations where I'm thinking, *All these people know what they're doing. They're highly experienced; I don't need to give them a checklist—and they don't want the extra task.* The client didn't have any checklists; they were a small company, so they didn't require it. And I was thinking, *everybody knows what they're doing. I'm not going to go through this exercise of training them on a checklist or mandate something that they know what they're doing.* Well, what do you think happened? When a protocol amendment went out to sites, it had "draft" in the header. Simple, basic checklist item. Everybody's busy, you're trying to meet the deadline, you're doing all these tasks, you have all these things in your head for all the other projects you have going on, or what you need to do for this particular project. Especially if you're under a time crunch, which we 99% are, there's no way you're going to remember everything and something like that is going to slip through. So it was just a wake-up call. I have got to have procedures, I have got to have checklists, and everybody's got to use them. That's how I run my business now. And that's a requirement for delivering high-quality documents. It's just foundational.

How long have you been using them?

It was probably about eight years ago when I first did a consulting gig, which was with a major biotech company, and of course, they had a lot of structure around what they did, even down to checklists and making sure QC [quality control] was done. I had to sign off that QC was completed for any project, and that everything was addressed. So everything was documented. In the event of an audit, they could see, *yes, it was done,* so there's a certain level of audit readiness or inspection readiness in place. So if somebody comes to see if you're following your own procedures, you can show through your documentation that it's done. As they say in research, "if it isn't documented, it didn't happen."

So in your current work, how many checklists do you think you have?

I have four right now. And those are the core documents that I typically work on. I imagine over time as we get into other document types, we'll keep adding to that. So right now it's mainly clinical study documents like investigator's brochures, protocols, protocol amendments, and CSRs. So I haven't expanded into submission document checklists yet because we're not doing that work right now, but that's an inevitable thing.

What is your process for putting together a new checklist?

How do you start? Good question. Usually I'll look for reference documents, if it's an old checklist that I had, and then looking through regulations to make sure all the regulatory components that need to be on the checklist are there. So, if there are required elements based on ICF [Informed Consent Form] or GCP [Good Clinical Practice], that those are there. And obviously, anything that relates to style or checking for consistency with the style guide. And we talked about headers and footers that are easy to overlook if you're in a rush. So, usually it's piecing those things together between reference style documents that I've used in the past, or my team has used in the past, and just making sure it's aligned with current regulations.

So would you say that you create checklists for a certain task for a certain client? Or do you just have one for certain tasks, and you just use it for all your clients?

That's a good question. Developing checklists and style guides so that clients can adopt them if they want and we can say, *This is what we use,* so that we're doing all the same thing if they don't want to put that in an SOP or don't have an SOP. I mean if you work with small companies, they're just not going to have it. And so I'll have them for my own team. This is what we use. This is how we get trained on the procedure that is affiliated with it and the checklist itself and say, *This is a mandatory thing and it's going to be signed.* Even if it's internal, so that we know it was done, just like I was mandated to do by larger companies. There's a really good reason why that's required. I remember going through this when I first started using checklists, I'm thinking, *Do I really need to do this? This seems like a wasted effort.* And you start going through it, and you realize, *Oh, I missed that, and I missed that, too.* And then you realize, this is really important. That's why you absolutely need to use the checklist, across the board. It's part of the process and supports quality and regulatory compliance.

I was reading about different kinds of checklists, and one is a read-do (in other words, read it, do it) and then the other one was a do-confirm (in other words, do it, confirm it). Do you ask people working for you to make sure they're checking it as they go (read-do) or do you just care they can check it after they thought they've done it (do-confirm)?

Oh you mean, check it against the checklist as you're writing the document. As long as it's checked at the end when it's all completed. That means to me that you'd have to check it again if you were changing things as you're going.

So the important thing is not to say, *Okay, well, I already checked that.* In the beginning, you probably changed your document enough where there's new elements and things have changed. So I wouldn't recommend to anybody to check it while they're doing it, but to certainly be aware of your checklist. Maybe I can save myself some work on the end by checking my hyperlinks now. If you know what's on your checklist, and that's top of mind, but inevitably at the end, you're going to want to go through it again just to make sure when everything is pretty final.

Before the final draft, before it gets submitted to QC, you want to make sure QC doesn't have to do your work for you, right? You see, they're there to check it. They're not there to fill in all that you omitted. So typically, at least in regulatory writing, I haven't heard of people checking against the checklist earlier than the final draft for the reasons I talked about. Unless it's just to make sure, *Hey, this is a top of mind that I'm gonna have to be checking these things.* So if I do them right initially, then I won't have to redo them or fix a lot of things at the end, right up against a deadline, that's all.

Another thing I try to think about is new versus experienced. Maybe as a new person, you are going to check the checklist a lot more to make sure you're catching everything, since you're still learning, you're still trying to get into your groove, whereas an experienced person, you actually have in your head that internalized checklist and you know what needs to be done. And so the checklist is really a double check, since you've probably done everything you need to do, but it's just making sure.

Yeah, I have a good analogy for that. I have done some rock climbing in the past, and they publish a book of accidents that happen at the end of every year so that other people can avoid them. And typically it's really basic things that really experienced people forget or think, *I don't have to worry about this because I know what I'm doing.* And if they had a checklist to tie a knot at the end of the rope, they wouldn't have somebody sliding off the end of it. You always tie a knot in the end of your rope. But if you're like, *I know what I'm doing, I just need to hurry up here. We don't have a lot of time; there's a storm coming in.* And it's usually something like that. You're under some kind of pressure or you're tired. And I think that analogy translates really well to medical writing. You're tired. Maybe you've been at it for a while. You're fatigued. Your brain is fatigued. And you think you know better: *I don't need to go through the checklist. I don't need to read the SOP. I know it. I've been doing this for twenty years. I don't need the crutch.* If you're new, then you definitely need the crutch. But honestly, experienced or not, you need it anyway. I've relearned to be very diligent in following standard operating procedures and the checklists that are associated with them. It's just too easy to forget something otherwise.

I think checklists are really important when you're new, but they're still important when you're experienced. And I think a lot of intermediate-level people, maybe they are getting along and they think they're getting along fine without a checklist, but I feel like it could take them to the next level sometimes if they do start using checklists.

Oh, absolutely. I mean, especially when I was a newbie, a checklist was a great tool to make sure that everything was covered. And, you know, I would go through them with a fine-tooth comb and make sure after I went through the checklist, I'd even look through it again to see if there's something I said to myself, *I'm going to do that later.* You know, actually check the checklist, check it off, and make sure you don't put a checkmark there until you've actually completed the whole thing. Even if it takes more time, because ultimately, that's your reputation. If you let something slide through, like what happened to me. My reputation was tainted because one of my team members didn't have a checklist and just thought they knew better. They said, *Well, it didn't really compromise patient safety or data integrity.* And I said, *No, that's a big egg on our face and reflects on us very poorly. It's our reputation.* And if we rely on referrals and testimonials and repeat business, then we can't have mistakes like that happen.

I am trying to differentiate basic versus comprehensive checklists. Would you consider yours basic or comprehensive when you look at the checklists that you have?

Definitely comprehensive. Like I said, these are tailored to specific document types that have specific components. And even though we do have a generic regulatory document checklist, that's for anything that's not under another umbrella. So as an example, we might do a pharmacy manual as a one-off. It's not something we normally do. The client asked for it. We're going to use a more generic checklist just to make sure we're hitting everything: did you update the table of contents before you submitted it? Did you do a spell check at the end? There's some basic stuff to make sure it's in good order.

If we're going to go the mountaineering analogy again, if you go camping, you're going to have a checklist. You need your tent, you need your stakes, you need all the food and the supplies and the gear for rain. It's a basic checklist. But if you're camping at base camp for Mount Everest, then you're talking about needing oxygen, you need crampons for the glaciers and for the ice; that's not normal camping. You need comprehensive checklists. So this is analogous to that. This is very specific. It's very high consequence in regulatory writing. So you don't want to miss regulatory components that absolutely need to be in there. And for us, we have document templates, normally that also have a lot of the required elements baked into them. But let's double-check to make sure: does this document comply with ICH [International Council for Harmonisation of Technical Requirements for Pharmaceuticals for Human Use] guidelines? Sure, your template should have it baked in, but did something new come up that we need to include? You still need to check it, even though we're trying to make it as foolproof as possible from the get-go. The checklist is there to make sure that all those things are covered, but you just can't assume that there is nothing new required.

What do you consider the benefits of using checklists in your work?

Yeah, it's kind of a summary of what we talked about. It's regulatory compliance, it's quality control, even though it's not QC, it's like a pre-QC step to make sure that document is the highest quality you can get it before the QC reviewer gets it. What else is it? It's compliance with company standard operating procedures and work instructions. And it's just doing, I call it a dummy check, but kind of tongue in cheek, but just to make sure that when things are in a fast-paced environment where you may be fatigued, you're not going to forget something silly like removing the work "draft" in the header. We need to make sure that all the dozens of things that we need to remember to do for our documents are actually done because it would otherwise be impossible to keep track of. So it's just to make sure that we're checking off all the boxes and dotting the Is and crossing the Ts.

How do you know you have good checklists?

Well, a lot of it comes with experience. And also, I guess the proof is in the pudding. When you're generating quality documents that don't get kicked back to you by the publishers. They will publish to regulatory standards to make sure everything is correct, and they'll check a lot of these things. They're not doing a QC, but they'll check tables of contents, pagination, borders, and styles. And so, we need to address issues if they kick it back. So if things aren't getting kicked back, that's the validation that things are good. If there's no issues ongoing, when documents go to sites or to regulatory authorities and there's no questions or comments that we're saying, *Oh, can't believe we missed that.*

So in clinical documents, it might be the clinical site who's giving you that feedback. You can get tons of questions because it doesn't make sense to the audience of the document. And it's not just checklists that go into that, but that is part of it.

Or if it's going to a regulatory agency, there might be more questions than would otherwise be there if we don't do a really good job and follow a checklist. So I think the proof is in the conduct of the study or the smoothness of the interactions with the health authority, whether it's FDA [Food and Drug Administration] or EMA [European Medicines Agency] or whoever else it might be. And that's the evidence of our quality in addition to sticking to timelines because we don't have to redo things or fix anything major.

Would you say you're a checklist user, a checklist fan, a checklist enthusiast, or a checklist specialist?

I'm going to go with specialist, for sure.

What advice do you have for others when it comes to creating and using checklists in medical communication?

So if you're someone who has a lot of experience, used a lot of checklists, maybe you're working with other clients that you're actively using them, it could be a really good model to pull that detail into your own checklists.

Another thing is that on the AMWA website, there are foundational checklists [see the Measures of Success Toolkit in the *References* chapter]. So if you're looking at the regulations, other models that you have, and reviewing them with QC people, you'll have a solid start.

For example, I have QC experts reviewing my checklist. So it's not a QC checklist, but what are the QC people going to be looking at so that we can make it so that the writer is taking care of those things in advance. Then it doesn't have to be more burden on the QC person and then potentially delay or overburden QC where they're going to miss stuff, too, because there's just too many things to fix in the document. It's going to take a lot of work to fix everything versus a clean document that you can kind of give an A to, but you need to tweak it a little bit. They might find that there are some things that are inconsistent or that need to be fixed for style. Then you can just clean it up fairly easily. Otherwise, you might be looking at multiple rounds. It goes to QC, and then it comes back to you, you have to fix things, and it goes back to them again. That kind of back and forth can kill your schedule. It comes back to project management, managing expectations, and setting and being firm on timelines.

The consequence of that is going to be that you're going to have more errors. You're going to put it to QC. You're not going to have time to check everything as thoroughly as you would have otherwise, because you know how it works. It's like you finish something up, you come back at two the next day, and you're like, *how did I not see all this stuff?* Because you come back to it with a fresh set of eyes. If you don't have the time to do that, then it's going to go to QC and the QC per person is going to be grumbling quite a bit because it's just a ton of work for them. And then ultimately it's going to affect the quality of the deliverable to the client or to the end user, which is not what you want to have.

You were talking about experienced folks, but do you have different advice for people who are newer?

It's very similar. When I was newer at dedicated medical writing, I would work with these checklists more throughout the process of writing versus just at the end. Because I would notice that I would miss a ton of things based on my checklist. I'm like, *Oh, my gosh, I forgot all these different things. And now it's going to be a ton of time. And I thought I was done and I'm not.* So I would say to take the advice that you were alluding to before, which is, you can look at it as you're writing and use that as a pre-checklist. To make sure you're doing things as you're developing them. So in a typical scenario, one of the big things for all of our protocol checklists, we have a schedule of assessments. It's got all the assessments and procedures that go through the course of the whole study. And as you can imagine, it is exhaustive. It's hard to follow even for the sites. And if the body of the text doesn't match or the study outline doesn't match that, then you're going to have all kinds of problems. Sites aren't going to know what to do and they're going to see the inconsistencies. If you're newer and you look at the checklist, and it says, *make sure the content matches the schedule of assessments table,* you don't know that takes a ton of time. So if you don't know that you're doing that until the very end, you're going to go, *Oh, this is going to take me days longer.* So as you're more experienced, that's just intuitive. But you might not realize that if you're newer.

It seems to me, of all the areas of medical communications, regulatory requires checklists from the get-go, and that it really needs them more, than other areas of medical communications. To me, it seems almost like aviation. If you're in aviation, you follow a checklist all day. There's no choice. So I almost feel like regulatory is the aviation of medical communications because you might get away without checklists in other kinds of medical communications, but in regulatory, you could really struggle without checklists.

Yeah, if you're just jumping in your car and you're low on gas, no problem. If you jump in your plane and you have passengers and you run out of fuel, and that's like, *Oh, we didn't check how much fuel was in the tank.* You have to make sure before you get off the ground, that all these safety components are taken care of. And I'm not a pilot, but I can only imagine what they have to go through. It's a good analogy…we need to make sure that we're not going to burden the people or the process that come after us. And so the consequences in rock climbing or flying are more severe than even medical writing, but they are serious consequences, nonetheless. Otherwise, you could slow down your submission and jeopardize the ultimate approval of your drug or the clinical trial you're working on. A lot of times sites won't enroll patients if the protocol is too confusing or burdensome and there's too many procedures or if the protocol is not clear, or we're not going to make it as easy as possible for them to enroll patients and collect the data. If we do our job well, they can do their job well and enroll patients and not make it more work for them.

And if one site or one audience member is asking a question, you can bet everybody else is going to have the same question. So even if they didn't catch it when they read it the first time. But then they read it again in practice and they go, *Wait, this doesn't work.* Or even those things that you might not even notice when you're reading, even if you're the end user for that document. Also, maybe you don't notice that things are abbreviated differently in different places, but it's going to throw you off, or the styles are off. Or the font is different over here. And maybe you don't even consciously notice, but that's going to throw you off when you are reading it. If you have a super clean document, you can tell. It's just easier to manage as a reader.

Your brain doesn't have to do extra work. It's already enough to digest with this very highly technical, highly detailed, and sometimes very unavoidably confusing content where you have to make it very clear, consistent, and as simple as possible using the most basic language you can. So, if you can do that, then it's going to make it better for everybody in the whole clinical development process.

SUMMARY

Ready to make a conscious effort to focus on quality? Using a checklist can be a culture change, FROM relying on your instinct and memory to get things done TO relying on documented systems and processes to ensure quality.

Here are some things to remember as you go out in the world to create your own comprehensive checklists.

First, these checklists are for you to use, so no one can tell you what they should look like, and your client or manager should not be creating them for you. **You need to create them for you**. If you do get a checklist from someone else that you are required to use, consider creating a supplemental checklist for your personal use that covers items specific to you or that allow you to get the benefits of a comprehensive checklist. For teams, you can create one as a team if there's a task you all do and you need to be consistent in how you do it, but you have to work on the checklists together so they work for all of you. A checklist should not be punitive or a necessary evil. A checklist is a tool in your toolbox to do your job better, with less strife and more peace of mind.

Second, you should be updating your checklists and changing them as your job or the task changes. Most people encounter change pretty regularly. There's always a new system, or a new task, or you learn that you were doing something wrong that you want to correct. There's always change, so change the checklist as you and the task changes.

Third, comprehensive checklists are great for editing tasks, but you can use them for research work, writing, social media work, speaking engagements, podcasts, and other business tasks. Any type of repeated task is a good candidate for a checklist. Go on and do it if you need checklists for other types of tasks.

Whether new, mid-level, or experienced, you can harness the power of checklists in your daily tasks as a medical communicator. If you are not using any checklists, give them a try with a task you do often, then try it again. And if you have checklists that you know could be better (bye, bye, basic checklists!), then go through the steps in the *How Do You Get Started?* chapter and create your new checklists (hello, comprehensive checklists!).

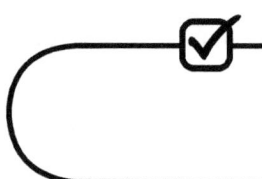

Questions? Ask! **Want personalized training?** Sign up!
Excited and want to share your checklists? Send them over!
Want me to come speak to your team or organization? Let's talk!
Email: checklist_specialist@headbookworm.com
Web: https://headbookworm.com/clarity-by-design/

REFERENCES

✓ American Medical Writers Association (AMWA). Measures of Success Toolkit. amwa.org. Member account required. Accessed August 4, 2025. https://www.amwa.org/general/custom.asp?page=Measures_of_Success.

✓ Bacon C. *Editing Scientific and Medical Research Articles.* Chartered Institute of Editing and Proofreading (CIEP); 2021.

✓ Christiansen S, Iverson C, Flanagin A, et al. *AMA Manual of Style: A Guide for Authors and Editors.* 11th ed. Oxford University Press; 2020.

✓ Elsevier. CRediT author statement. elsevier.com. Accessed September 8, 2025. https://www.elsevier.com/researcher/author/policies-and-guidelines/credit-author-statement

✓ Franzen A. *The Checklist Book: Set Realistic Goals, Celebrate Tiny Wins, Reduce Stress and Overwhelm, and Feel Calmer Every Day.* TMA Press; 2020.

✓ Gawande A. *The Checklist Manifesto: How to Get Things Right.* Henry Holt & Company; 2010.

✓ Higgins WY, Boorman DJ. An analysis of the effectiveness of checklists when combined with other processes, methods and tools to reduce risk in high hazard activities. *Boeing Tech J.* 2016. https://www.boeing.com/content/dam/boeing/boeingdotcom/features/innovation-quarterly/2019_q3/BTJ_checklist_full.pdf

✓ Power S. 5 benefits of adopting patient safety checklists. Physician-Patient Alliance for Health & Safety. ppahs.org. https://ppahs.org/2013/03/5-benefits-of-adopting-patient-safety-checklists/

✓ Rizzo P. *Listful Thinking: Using Lists to be More Productive, Highly Successful and Less Stressed.* Start Midnight, LLC; 2014.

✓ Sarcevic A, Zhang Z, Marsic I, Burd RS. Checklist as a memory externalization tool during a critical care process. *AMIA Annu Symp Proc.* 2017;2016:1080-1089.

✓ Schrank K. Using editing checklists for more efficient editing. *AMWA J.* 2013(4):164-166. https://cdn.ymaws.com/www.amwa.org/resource/resmgr/journal/Issues/2013/2013v28n4_online.pdf

CHECKLIST EXAMPLES

The following pages have examples of checklists that I use or have used in the past, along with some examples from Alexandra Howson and Crystal Herron, who have generously shared their checklists:

- ✓ Check Changes Checklist
- ✓ CME Writing Project Scope Checklist
- ✓ Dossier Checklist
- ✓ Financial Friday Checklist
- ✓ Manuscript Checklists
- ✓ Marketing Monday Checklist
- ✓ Slide Deck Checklists
- ✓ Speaking Engagements Checklist
- ✓ Standard Response Checklist
- ✓ YouTube Video Checklist

They are a mix of business checklists, like the Financial Friday checklist that might be helpful for freelancers; medical communication task checklists that might be helpful to those who work in manuscripts, and professional checklists, like the speaking engagement checklist, which might be helpful for those who are sharing their skills and experience with others professionally.

On my website, you can download copies of my checklists: https://headbookworm.com/checklist-examples/

CHECK CHANGES CHECKLIST

This is one of my medical communication checklists.

A check changes task for an editor working in promotional/advertising materials in the pharmaceutical industry is when you check the new copy against a previous copy that is marked up with changes needed. Both documents are usually PDFs, and changes are in comments and annotations. There might be multiple rounds if questionable edits are requested or the designer misunderstands the instructions.

This checklist is meant to be printed out, so there are four columns of blank boxes to the left of the items for the checkmarks to account for the multiple rounds of review. Likewise, there are multiple slots to add in timing (start and stop times). Time is counted in 15-minute intervals, so the time spent usually says, 1, for one hour, or 15, meaning 15 minutes, or any other combination of numbers depending on how long it takes.

In this task, you are looking, first and foremost, to make sure the changes marked up were made by the designer, but you are also looking for issues that might have arisen when the changes were made. Is all of the text that was in the previous version in the new version (InDesign is notorious for letting text be cut off when new text is added)? Did the markup have a misspelling that the designer copied and pasted into the InDesign file? If the answer to these questions is yes, you need to mark the issues to be fixed in the next version. Did the designer add a page to a document with a table of contents? You'll have to make sure the changes didn't affect the page numbers in the table of contents. If it's digital material, you need to make sure that changes were made consistently to both the mobile and desktop version.

Check Changes
Checklist

			Receive new PDF proof and mark-up PDF via email
			Save new PDF proof with initials
			Ensure all directions in email have been followed
			Ensure all changes directed in markup have been made
			Edit changes
			Mark up edits/comments on the new PDF proof
			Address any requests from the designer
			Conduct a side-by-side proofread of content: • Color • Font style (italic/bold)
			Ensure the following do not break over lines: • Generic name (BRAND NAME) or vice versa
			Split screen to check the Mobile against the Desktop • ALL CAPS always ALL CAPS • Count all footnotes in both versions • Check periods at end of each footnotes • Check spacing in drop-down text (before and after separator)
			Insert a **Reviewed** stamp if there are changes to be made or an **Approved** stamp if there are no changes
			Insert time into timesheet
			Reply All when returning

Details:

Job Number: _____

Date: _____ Due: _____

Start time: _____ _____ _____

Stop time: _____ _____ _____

Time spent: _____ _____ _____

CME WRITING PROJECT SCOPE CHECKLIST

Alexandra Howson shared this checklist for CME writers. Her introduction says that users can "Use this checklist before every CME writing project to set clear expectations, prevent scope creep, and establish healthy business boundaries."

CME Writing Project Scope Checklist

☑ Use this checklist before every CME writing project to set clear expectations, prevent scope creep, and establish healthy business boundaries.

1. Project Overview

- [ ] Client and project lead identified
- [ ] Activity type defined (needs assessment, enduring module, outcomes report, live event content, etc.)
- [ ] Delivery format confirmed (slides, script, article, online module, etc.)
- [ ] Target audience documented (specialty, role, practice setting)

2. Deliverables

- [ ] Draft learning objectives aligned with identified gaps
- [ ] Content outline or storyboard
- [ ] Script, slides, or article content (specify format + word count/slide count)
- [ ] Assessment items (number and type specified: MCQs, polling, case-based, etc.)
- [ ] Reference list in agreed format (AMA, APA, etc.)
- [ ] Outcomes reporting content (if applicable: survey items, short summary narrative)

3. Out-of-Scope Items *(clarify early to prevent scope creep)*

- ☐ Graphic design and formatting
- ☐ Video production or editing
- ☐ Raw data collection or statistical analysis
- ☐ SME recruitment or scheduling
- ☐ Grant portal formatting or submission

4. Workflow & Timelines

- ☐ Project start and delivery dates agreed
- ☐ SME interview schedule confirmed (who schedules, who attends, recording/transcript availability)
- ☐ Number of revision rounds included (e.g., 2–3)
- ☐ Turnaround expectations for client feedback (e.g., 5 business days)
- ☐ Escalation plan if deadlines are at risk

5. Business Terms

- ☐ Agreed pricing model (hourly, project-based, or retainer)
- ☐ Proposal/scope approved in writing
- ☐ Payment terms and schedule confirmed (deposit, milestones, final payment)
- ☐ Late fee policy included (if applicable)
- ☐ Rush or weekend surcharge agreed (if applicable)

6. Communication & Systems

- ☐ Primary communication channel (email, PM tool, client platform)
- ☐ File naming and version control system agreed
- ☐ Feedback process clarified (tracked changes, comments in slides, centralized doc, etc.)

7. Intellectual Property & Portfolio Use

- [ ] Content ownership and usage rights defined
- [ ] Permission for de-identified samples in your portfolio clarified
- [ ] Confidentiality and non-disclosure terms agreed

8. Professional Boundaries

- [ ] Working hours and availability defined
- [ ] Expected response times agreed (e.g., 24–48 hours)
- [ ] Policy for urgent or weekend requests clarified

> **Want a step-by-step process and support as you launch and grow in CME? Join us!**
>
> If you're ready for clear guidance and support as you work on your 2026 goals and projects, WriteCME Pro is here for you! We are a community for ambitious writers who are focusing on building a sustainable niche in CME writing.
>
> Learn more and join us here →

DOSSIER CHECKLIST

This is one of my medical communication checklists.

An Academy of Managed Care Pharmacy (AMCP) formulary dossier is a popular type used in the US for pharmaceutical products. They are often created by folks with PharmDs or PhDs in Medical Information or Medical Affairs in the pharmaceutical or medical devices industry. There are commercial dossiers, global value dossiers, and dossiers for medical devices, which are less common and might look similar but do not follow this format. Like many documents in the pharmaceutical industry, dossiers are often put together by different teams of writers, often leading to inconsistency in format and presentation of content. Certain sections repeat content, so edits need to ensure content stays consistent.

Editing a dossier can be a lengthy endeavor; the shortest can be 50 pages, but the longest are closer to 300 pages. This editing checklist for an AMCP dossier is long and allows for a bit more leeway in its formatting. Most companies have one formulary dossier for each drug and some have a second shorter one for Medicaid, so while it's a lot of work when it's being updated once a year, there's no year-long flow of work on dossiers in most companies.

Editor Checklist
Dossier

Instructions	
Use this checklist for dossiers that need a standard edit.	

Owner: _____ Product: _____ Editor: _____

Date Received: _____ Date Due: _____ Rush: Yes No Dossier#: _____

Approve/Activate: Yes No   Track Changes: Yes No   # of Pages: _____

Time: _____ _____ _____   Date Completed: _____   Entered in Tracker: _____
    START STOP SPENT

CHECK OUT DOCUMENT
FORMATTING
Check Margins: 1" on top, bottom, left, and right
Check Footer: Left side should say: Section X.X or References or Abbreviations   Right side should have auto-pagination: Page X of X
Check for Keep with Next near headings and tables
Check that spacing between paragraphs is consistent: spaces (¶) or consistent spacing before and after (3pt/6 pt).
Check Bulleted and Numbered Lists   Make sure bullets and numbers begin at the left margin and that the tab is only .25 for each level.
Check Size of Font   • Body Text: 10 pt Times New Roman   • Headings: 12 pt Times New Roman
Check Justification   • Check that body text, bullets, and references are left justified.
Check Spacing   • Do a Find for period followed by 2 spaces; replace with period followed by 1 space.   • Do a Find for 2 spaces; replace with 1 space..
Check Headings and Sections of Document: Look for consistency in heading levels, order of sections, and use of bullets.   **2.2 HEADING LEVEL 1**: Bold, Small Caps   2.2.1 HEADING LEVEL 2: Roman, Small Caps   2.2.1.1 Heading Level 3: Roman, Initial Caps   (no number) Heading Level 4: Underlined, Initial Caps   (no number) *Heading Level 5*: Italics, Initial Caps   (no number) Heading Level 6: Roman, Initial Caps
ABBREVIATIONS
Check Abbreviations and Acronyms   • Ensure that there are no periods in abbreviations (*Examples*: ie, US) (*Exception*: vs.).   • Ensure abbreviations and acronyms are used consistently within the dossier   • Use abbreviations and acronyms only if the term is used ≥3 times in the document.   **Note**: If using Find and Replace to help locate abbreviations and acronyms, be sure to look for both the abbreviation and the spelled-out version.   • Headings should have full version in most cases.   • Abbreviations are included in a separate list; some dossiers will not spell out on first mention, others do. Follow whatever system they have established.

Editor Checklist
Dossier

CROSS-REFERENCES AND ENDNOTES
Not all dossiers have endnotes and cross-references, but if they do, please check the following:
- Count references; ensure that they are in the correct order at first presentation.
- Check that endnotes show a reference when you hover over them and that citation information provided matches reference endnote (where applicable).
- Check that cross-references show a link when you hover over them.
- Make sure all endnote and cross-reference numbers, ®, and ™ are superscript without spaces between them and the word preceding them.
- Make sure all endnote and cross-reference numbers are the same font size as surrounding text.

TABLES/FIGURES
Tables/Figures
- Count tables and figures; tables and figures should be numbered consecutively with bold capital roman numerals (*Example:* **I, II, III, IV, V**).
- "TABLE" and "FIGURE" should be ALL CAP and bold (*Example:* **TABLE I, FIGURE II**).
- Ensure that a colon and 2 spaces follow the table/figure number, that the table/figure title is bold and Initial Caps, and that the title ends with a period (*Example:* **TABLE I: Title Title Title.**)
- Ensure there is an "Adapted from" line (not bold) or an endnote/cross-reference after the title.
- Ensure footnotes are indicated with superscript lowercase letters in alphabetical order (a-z).

Tables
- Highlight each table:
    - Table Tools/Design, click Table Grid. Check that formatting/shading has not been lost.
    - Table Tools/Layout/Properties, check that table is left aligned and that indent from left is 0.1."
- Make sure units of measure in tables are specified in column headings or sub-headings, but not duplicated in cells.
- Make sure text in header row and any shaded rows is bold and initial cap; however, text/data within the columns should be sentence case and not bold.
- If a table is very long and has to break between 2 pages, ensure that header rows are repeated.

STYLE
Check Capitalization in Headings and Sub-Headings
Capitalize:
- Nouns, pronouns, verbs, adjectives, and adverbs, the first word after a colon, and the first and last words
- Prepositions of ≥ four letters (With, From, Into, Onto)

Do NOT Capitalize:
- Articles and coordinating conjunctions (and, or, but)
- Prepositions of ≤ three letters (eg, in, on, for)

Check Global Wording Changes
- Check that "Prescribing Information" is only used with product name.
- Check that "labeling information" is used in generic mentions.
- Check that "complete product information" is changed to "further product information."
- Change instances of "and colleagues" to "et al."

Check Numbers
- Numerals should be used to express numbers as opposed to spelling out numbers
- Numbers that begin a sentence should always be spelled out

Check Symbols and Signs
- Ensure the appropriate use and format of symbols and signs within parentheses and in tables/figures.
- Ensure that symbols and signs are spelled out in text, except for lab values (*Examples:* CK >10x ULN; HbA1c ≥6.5%; BMI ≥25 kg/m^2).

Check Units of Measure
- Ensure the appropriate format of units of measure.

CHECKLIST EXAMPLES 91

Editor Checklist
Dossier

REFERENCES	
Check References Section: Two different formats are used, so edit accordingly.	
References Citations should be at the end of the sentence. Example: Text (Name 2011).	
Standard References List: Ensure references are lined up on the left and the hanging indent is 0.13″. • **Journal articles** should follow the following example: Ando T, Ishikawa T, Kokura S, et al. Endoscopic analysis of gastric ulcer after one week's treatment with omeprazole and rabeprazole. *Dig Dis Sci*. 2008;53:933-937. • **Web references** can be more complicated but look for the following: Brown RW, O'Brien CD, Martin UJ, et al. Long-term safety and asthma control measures with a budesonide/formoterol pressurized metered-dose inhaler in African American asthmatic patients: a randomized controlled trial [published online ahead of print April 30 2012]. *J Allergy Clin Immunol*. 2012. http://dx.doi.org/10.1016/j.jaci.2012.03.028. Accessed February 15, 2013.	
Edit Dossier	
FINAL TOUCHES	
Run Spell Check	
Update Fields for Cross-references	
Change View to 100% and Look it Over One More Time	
Save Document	
CHECK DOCUMENT BACK IN	
Check Rendition in Viewer • Refresh page • Open in Full Screen • Look for endnotes and cross-references coming in at a different size than the rest of the text or cross-references coming in not superscripted	
Complete the Task • Click **Complete**. ○ Click **Approved** if the instructions were to edit and activate and you have no questions. ○ Click **Approved** if the instructions were to edit and track changes and other reviewers are included in the review cycle. ○ Click **Not Approved** if the instructions were to edit and activate but you have questions. • Leave a comment at the bottom of the document. • Email the author. • Check expiration date. Click **Complete**.	

FINANCIAL FRIDAY CHECKLIST

This is one of my business checklists.

The focus of the task is to keep up with the financials of your business. Freelancers often struggle with this aspect of having their own business, so it's a motivational checklist more than a procedural one because the order is less important. You might have more sophisticated systems, and if you do, by all means use their functionality to keep up with all this. But if you're too new to even know what you need to do yet or what systems you need, this might be a good start for you.

FINANCIAL FRIDAY CHECKLIST
Tasks to keep finances top of mind

Date: _____

Check Bank
- ☐ Balance – Checking   _____
- ☐ Balance – Savings   _____
- ☐ Balance – Credit Card   _____

- ☐ Other bills coming up?
  - $_____ for _____
  - $_____ for _____
  - $_____ for _____
  - $_____ for _____
  - $_____ for _____
  - $_____ for taxes (April, June, September, January)

Check on Invoices

		Current	Unpaid Invoice(s)	Need to Invoice	Need to Finish Project
☐					
☐					
☐					
☐					
☐					
☐					
☐					
☐					
☐					
☐					
☐					
☐					
☐					

Prep for Taxes
When checking, savings, and credit card statements come, annotate with categories and send to accountant.

MANUSCRIPT CHECKLISTS

Here are two manuscript editing checklists: the first one is from me and the second one is from Crystal Herron. A manuscript writing project checklist from Alexandra Howson is also included here.

I shared my checklist at many conferences and webinars. Using the advice provided in those sessions, Crystal Herron used my checklist to get her checklist started and then made it her own. These manuscript checklists show how starting with the same template, people can make their own versions in order to make it work for them. These are meant for use when you're editing manuscripts for scientific or medical journals, and mine is walked through in the case study.

The third one is completely different: a manuscript writing project start-up checklist from Alexandra Howson. Her introduction says that users can "Use this checklist to support manuscript project start-up."

Editor Checklist
Manuscript

Client: _____ Project # _____ Additional Contact: _____

Manuscript (long title): _____

_____

Manuscript (short title): _____

Journal (name): _____ Journal (abbreviation): _____

Instructions to Authors site: _____

Date Due: _____ Pages: _____ Refs: _____ Figures: _____ Tables: _____

Time: ____ ____ ____   Time: ____ ____ ____   Time: ____ ____ ____
     START STOP SPENT   START STOP SPENT   START STOP SPENT

Time: ____ ____ ____   Time: ____ ____ ____   Time: ____ ____ ____
     START STOP SPENT   START STOP SPENT   START STOP SPENT

	Run PerfectIt
	Edit title page Ensure it has everything required from journal
	Clean up author section • Ensure consistent names, titles, affiliations, and locations • Ensure there is contact information for lead or corresponding author on cover page • Ensure there is contact information for all authors (if needed for submission)
	Edit abstract Make sure it has the following sections (or similar as required by journal): • Background • Methods • Results • Conclusion **Count number of words and compare to journal requirements:** Journal Req: _____ Abstract: _____
	Count number of keywords and compare to journal requirements: Journal Req: _____ Main text: _____
	Edit keywords
	Edit main text Make sure it has the following sections: • Introduction • Methodology • Results and Discussion (consider whether strict separation of these sections is important) • Conclusion
	Count number of words and compare to journal requirements: Journal Req: _____ Main text: _____
	Count number of figures and compare to journal requirements: Journal Req: _____ Manuscript: _____
	Ensure figures are the right format and size
	Count number of tables and compare to journal requirements: Journal Req: _____ Manuscript: _____
	Ensure tables follow journal requirements

Updated March 12, 2023   Courtesy of Kelly Schrank (headbookworm.com)   Page **1** of **2**

Editor Checklist
Manuscript

Check/Fix Abbreviations and Acronyms • Ensure that the composite words of abbreviations and acronyms are spelled out on first use in body text, followed by the abbreviation and/or acronym in parentheses. *Headings should have full version in most cases.* • Use abbreviations and acronyms only if the term is used ≥3 times in the document. Note: If using Find and Replace to help locate abbreviations and acronyms, look for both the spelled-out versions and the abbreviations. • Make sure that abbreviations and acronyms are used consistently within the manuscript.	
Count number of refs and compare to journal requirements: Journal Req: Main text:	
Edit references • Look up each reference and correct if needed • Edit according to journal's author instructions and *AMA Manual of Style*	
Edit supplementary materials	
Edit conflict of interest statements / funding statements / disclosures	
Edit CRediT author statement	
Edit Acknowledgements Make sure you are acknowledged as appropriate	
Notes from Journal's Author Instructions	
Additional materials needed	

FINAL TOUCHES	
Run spell check	
Run PerfectIt	
Turn off track changes	
Change View to 100% • Look over one more time in **All Markup** • Reread comments to ensure they are still needed and worded appropriately • Look over one more time in **No Markup**	
Save Document	
Email back to author in email subject line that matches naming convention	
WHEN READY TO SUBMIT	
Edit cover letter	
Ensure that author order and affiliations in system matches manuscript	
Ask authors to provide any conflicts of interest statements / funding statements / disclosures	
Ask if they have suggested reviewers or not-suggested reviewers (if provided in submission system)	
Confirm manuscript type	
Ensure you have all of the appropriate files to upload • Ensure cover letter and manuscript are together or separate as indicated in journal instructions • Ensure figures are separate files (or not) as required	

Editor Checklist
Original Research Manuscript

Client: _____

Title: _____

Journal (name): _____

Article Type: _____ Date Due: _____ Editing level: _____

First Touches
- Add to Project CV
- Create cover sheet

Initial Formatting
Format document
- Add template and apply styles
- Headings
  - Level 1: All caps, bold, new line
  - Level 2: Sentence case, bold, new line
  - Level 3: Sentence case, bold, same line
- New line for new paragraphs, indent
- Font requirement: _____
- Margins: 1" all around
- Page/line numbers: _____

Format title page
- Title
- Short title
- Authors
- Affiliations, space between superscript and text
- Corresponding author info

Content
Edit abstract
Make sure discusses the following topics:
- Background
- Purpose/objective
- Methods
- Results
- Conclusions

Edit keywords

Edit main text
Make sure has the following sections:
- Introduction
- Methods
- Results
- Discussion
- Conclusions

Check statements
- IRB/IACUUC approval
- Informed consent

Edit back matter

Edit supplementary materials

Tables and Figures
Review tables
- Titles
  - Title case
  - No punctuation at end
- Headings
  - Sentence case
  - Units after comma, no in parentheses
- Cells
  - Sentence case
- Table notes
  - Footnotes: superscript letters, space between superscript and text
  - Abbreviations: use lead text
  - Order: Abbreviations. Footnotes.
- Format
  - No shading, use thick lines to separate sections
  - All columns left-aligned

Review figures
- Titles
  - Title case
  - No punctuation at end if no description
- Legends
  - Order: Title. Description. Abbreviations.
  - Abbreviations: no lead text
- Layout/design
  - Sentence case text
  - Labels
  - Error bars for graphs
  - Scales for imaging
  - Clarity

Numbering and callouts
- Check numbering is correct
- Check callouts are correct

Final Formatting

Check abbreviations
- Use abbreviations if terms used ≥3 times
- Define on first use
- Do not use in headings

Check statistics
- Check format of P values
- Check spacing around mathematical symbols (eg, non-breaking)
- Check spacing of units
- Stats formatting: [odds ratio (OR), 3.1; 95% CI, 2.2-4.8; P = .0321]

Edit references and citations
- Look up each reference and correct
- Keep hyperlinks for urls
- Edit according to journal style
- Format citations

Notes	Snippets

Final Touches

Final Review
- Accept formatting changes
- Review comments
- Run spell check
- Update cover sheet

Manuscript Project Start-Up Checklist

Use this checklist to support manuscript project start-up.

▸ Table of contents

▾ Assess the project complexities

- ☐ Gather essential project details from your client during a discovery call
- ☐ Ask questions to help clients articulate their needs and expectations
- ☐ Assess topic difficulty and specialization
- ☐ Target audience (general practitioners vs. specialists)
- ☐ Required research depth
- ☐ Number and complexity of graphics/tables needed
- ☐ Audience for manuscript

▼ Estimate time requirements

- [ ] Literature review and research
  - Does the client have a reference library?
  - Has the client drafted a framework for the manuscript?
  - Will you need to search and synthesize the literature to support the introduction and discussion?
- [ ] Outlining and planning
- [ ] Reference formatting
- [ ] Writing and revising
- [ ] Incorporating feedback
- [ ] Creating visuals and tables
- [ ] Formatting and references
- [ ] Familiarize yourself with the specific journal requirements
- [ ] Account for time needed to format manuscripts according to these guidelines

▼ Consider additional factors

- [ ] Deadline urgency
- [ ] Client's reputation and potential for future work
- [ ] Your expertise in the specific field
- [ ] Factor in time for potential revisions after peer review
- [ ] Obtain necessary permissions for use of copyrighted material
- [ ] Be prepared for follow-up questions or requests for additional information post-submission

▼ Develop a pricing structure

- [ ] Hourly rate vs. per-project fee
- [ ] Word count-based pricing
- [ ] Tiered pricing based on complexity
- [ ] Price based on the value your work provides to the client

Account for overhead costs

- Software and research tools
- Professional development and CME credits
- Business expenses (insurance, taxes, etc.)

1. Research market rates:

- Survey fellow medical writers
- Consult professional organizations like AMWA or EMWA
- Analyze job postings for similar projects

1. Create a detailed scope of work:

- Clearly outline deliverables
- Specify number of revisions included
- Define milestones and deadlines

1. Build in contingencies:

- Allow for unexpected complexities
- Include a buffer for additional client requests

1. Consider value-based pricing:

- Price based on the value your work provides to the client
- Factor in your expertise and unique selling points

1. Develop a questionnaire for clients:

- Use it to gather essential project details
- Help clients articulate their needs and expectations

1. Offer package deals:

- Bundle services (e.g., writing, editing, formatting)
- Provide discounts for long-term or multiple-project commitments

1. Regularly review and adjust your pricing:

- As you gain experience and expertise
- To reflect changes in the market and your skills

Would you like me to elaborate on any of these points or discuss a specific aspect of scoping and pricing for CME manuscript writing?

▼ **Create a detailed scope of work**
- ☐ Clearly outline deliverables
- ☐ Specify number of revisions included
- ☐ Define milestones and deadlines
- ☐ Build in contingencies
  - Allow for unexpected complexities
  - Include a buffer for additional client requests

MARKETING MONDAY CHECKLIST

This is one of my business checklists.

Like the Financial Friday checklist, this checklist has alliteration to make it more fun and memorable and provides some motivation for another task many freelancers dislike. You can use this to remind you of the things you could be doing to move your business forward, track when you contact connections or potential clients, and give yourself a little pat on the back that you got something done. The checklist can be updated with new types of tasks on a regular basis. For example, you might not update your profiles on professional association websites every week, but this reminds you to do it sometimes. In a busy week, you might not do it, but on a slower week, you might look at a profile on a platform and make sure it's optimized.

MARKETING MONDAY

A weekly plan to keep marketing my services on a regular basis

Week: _____

Email Marketing

Email current clients to check in

☐ _____ ☐ _____ ☐ _____
      Name   Name   Name

Notes:

Email prospects

☐ _____ ☐ _____ ☐ _____
      Name   Name   Name

Notes:

Email professional contacts for referrals, recommendations, or testimonials

☐ _____ ☐ _____ ☐ _____
      Name   Name   Name

Notes:

Social Media

	Mon	Tues	Wed	Thurs	Fri
Check LinkedIn for things to like or share	☐	☐	☐	☐	☐
Post something to social media	☐	☐	☐	☐	☐
Post that I am available	☐	☐	☐	☐	☐

Networking

Email network to stay in touch

☐ _____ ☐ _____ ☐ _____
      Name   Name   Name

Notes:

Email network to stay in touch

☐ _____ ☐ _____ ☐ _____
      Name   Name   Name

Notes:

Calls with Network

☐ _____ _____ _____
      Name   Date   Place

LinkedIn
☐ Go through notifications of recent job moves in pharma and follow up with folks

☐ _____   ☐ _____   ☐ _____
       Name   Name   Name

Notes:

☐ Post to website:
☐
☐

☐ Go through electronic files for TO DOs

Check Job Lists
☐ Check AMWA job list

☐ Check EFA job list

☐ Check LinkedIn jobs

☐ Check CSE job list

☐ Update profiles on professional association website

SLIDE DECK CHECKLISTS

These are two of my medical communication checklists.

Medical communications are frequently presented as slide decks created in PowerPoint. They can be used for a variety of audiences and purposes and range from a few pages to hundreds of pages long.

The first checklist in this section is an editing checklist, and the second is a quality check (QC) checklist.

The first checklist is landscape because the slide decks are also landscape orientation. It starts with the usual tracking information, but it discusses items in language specific to a slide, like where the slide number is located, where the trademark can go, and what is in the references. Some of the steps are abbreviated, with the assumption that the person using them (me) knew what that meant. At the time that worked for me, but earlier in editing slide decks, they would have been longer, with much more spelled out.

In the second checklist, we were QC'ing PowerPoint presentations that had been converted from one PowerPoint template to another. In this project, we would have to take old PowerPoints that had been created in an old style and convert them to a new template. If the person or team (as is often the case) had used a template, converting the slides to the new template was a breeze. But there were so many more that were never based on a template, making it manual labor. And there were *so* many of them, and the editors were a good choice for the work because we are detail oriented and systematic. But we still needed the checklist to help us get through it and to be sure we were consistent in our approach.

Editor Checklist
Editing of Slide Decks

Owner: _____	Title: _____		Editor: _____	Rush: Yes No	Date Received: _____
Due Date: _____	# of Slides: _____	Asset #: _____	Date: _____	Time: ___ ___ ___ START STOP SPENT	Entered in Tracker: _____

Time: ___ ___ ___ START STOP SPENT	Time: ___ ___ ___ START STOP SPENT	Time: ___ ___ ___ START STOP SPENT	Time: ___ ___ ___ START STOP SPENT

Use this checklist for editing slide decks in Vault. We have a 5-day turnaround for these; try to meet the deadline.

Make annotations in Vault. Preface each annotation with OPTIONAL or REQUIRED. When addressing an inconsistency or "error" that is repeated, make an annotation at the first instance, and add GLOBAL to beginning (after OPTIONAL or REQUIRED).

Strive to justify edits with that style is in template, guiding principles, or guidance.

It might be helpful to download the source document PDF to zoom up closer on small text, but annotations must be made in Vault.

Open the PDF and click through the decks to compare what's on each slide for the following:	
	Check Cover Sheet and Title Page: Be sure asset title reflects new naming convention: MARP <BRAND or TA> <Title> <full Vault asset #> *Examples:* MARP Symbicort pMDI RWE COPD Slide Deck ML-3010-US-0031 MARP Metabolics Role of Glucose Excursions ML-4006-US-0175
	Check Header: *Branded Decks* • Ensure that Product Names is in header • Ensure that Product Name is consistent throughout deck. **Note:** For branded slide decks containing disease state information, the brand and generic name should be removed from the header of each unbranded disease state slides. *Unbranded Decks* • Ensure there is nothing in header and that there is nothing throughout deck.
	Check Slide Numbers in left corner of slide
	Check logo in right corner of slide

Editor Checklist
Editing of Slide Decks

	Check disclaimer page: • Correct brand names • Extraneous information (investigational information when it's not)	
	Read Headings • Left-justified • Initial caps	
	Check Capitalization	
	Check Bulleted Lists	
	Check Font & Size	
	Check Justification • Left-justified	
While editing each slide, look for the following:		
	Check Numbers	
	Check Symbols and Signs	
	Check Units of Measure	
	Make sure registered trademarks are included on first use in deck; they do not need to be repeated at every mention	
	Check References • Abbreviated version of citation should be on slide • Make sure that all references in notes are on slide if there is an end note on the slide • Make sure placement of references on slide is consistent across slides	
Check Abbreviations		
Abbreviations Used		
Terminology Used		
Do NOT edit Notes pages, Backup slides, or slides that say DIRECT LIFT		
	Edit each slide	
	Annotate edits	
	When done annotating edits, press Complete.	
	Other Notes:	

Slide Deck QC Checklist

Brand: _____ Title: _____ Due Date: _____ # of Pages: ___

Editor: _____ Date: _____ Time: _____ _____ _____ Entered in Spreadsheet: _____
                                        START STOP SPENT

Use this checklist for the following: QC a slide deck conversion	
Open the New PowerPoint	
Make sure Cover Sheet is filled out	
Make sure Brand Name is on Disclaimer Page:	
Title Page: Make sure it is the purple title page, with brand name and asset number and date	
Content Master Page: Make sure brand name is 16 pt Arial (body), Roman	
Delete Slide Masters from Existing PowerPoint	
Check for Correct Master Slides • Medical Resources Content Master Slide Master (has AZ logo) • **NOT** Medical Resources Other Master Slide Master (no AZ logo)	
Look for Missing Text in Content, Tables, and Charts/Graphs	
Check Headings They should be 30 pt Arial, left justified, black, Initial caps There should be a purple line beneath them	
Check Bulleted Lists	
• **First level**	First level, bullet: 28 pt, Dark Purple, Accent 1
– Second level	Second level, en dash: 24 pt, Aqua Accent 2
▪ Third level	Third level, square: 20 pt, Lime, Accent 3
• Fourth level	Fourth level, bullet: 16 pt, Red, Accent 5
Check Font and Size (where possible, follow these standards) Text (not bullets): 28 pt, Arial (body), black In tables: 18 pt, Arial (body), black References: 10 pt, Arial (body), black	
Check Endnotes Make sure there is a space between the text and endnotes Make sure all asterisks are NOT superscript	
Check Coloring of Tables, Charts/Graphs, Smart Art	
Check that tables are similar to sample:	*(sample table shown)*

Assay	Agonist	Advantages	Disadvantages
VerifyNow®	Aspirin assay: arachidonic acid P2Y12 assay: ADP + PGE1 GP IIb/IIIa assay: TRAP	Rapid, user-friendly, high reproducibility, best-evaluated point-of-care assay	Not adjustable, rather expensive, no shear stress applied, results correlate with platelet count and red and white blood cells
VASP	PGE1 and PGE1 + ADP	Specificity towards P2Y12, low blood volume needed, sample storage is possible	Time consuming, expensive (requires flow cytometer), expertise required, insensitive to low levels of receptor blockade
Multiplate®	Arachidonic acid, collagen, ADP, TRAP	Rapid, duplicate measurements, user-friendly, adjustable	Only semi-automatic, manual agonist preparation and pipetting, long incubation of blood sample, results correlate with platelet count and red and white blood cells

Slide Deck QC Checklist

Check Bar Graphs Colors				
	Primary Color: Dark Purple, Accent 1	Secondary Color: Red, Accent 5	Tertiary Color: Aqua, Accent 2	Quarternary Color: Lime, Accent 3
	Primary should be used for AZ Brand	Secondary can be used for major competitor		
Check Line Charts Colors				
	Primary Color: Dark Purple, Accent 1	Secondary Color: Red, Accent 5 Darker 25%	Tertiary Color: Aqua, Accent 2 Darker 25%	Quarternary Color: Lime, Accent 3 Darker 50%
Check text boxes for References and Abbreviations/Footnotes • Delete "CI = confidence interval" if found in Abbreviations text box. • Abbreviations should only be defined once in the slide deck, on slide with first mention. • "Definition" does not need to be in content; abbreviation only needs to be defined in Abbreviations text box. • Delete spaces around equal marks; use equal marks instead of commas. • Insert a line break in long URLs (shift-Enter).				
Check Slide Animation • Advance Slide>On Mouse Click				
Check to make sure "Speaker Notes Disclaimer" are at the bottom of Notes page: • "Speaker notes are for internal use only and are not to be shown or disseminated outside of AstraZeneca."				

Change View and Look it Over One More Time
 • Slide Show
     o Check all links
 • Notes Page view
     o Make sure there is NOT >1 text box for notes
     o Adjust font size and text box size to make it fit on the page
 • Slide Sorter				

Compare the two decks side by side				
Save latest converted version to Sharepoint (and check it in)				
Email other editor that it has been QC'd				
Notes:				

SPEAKING ENGAGEMENTS CHECKLIST

This is one of my professional checklists.

As I began to have more speaking engagements in the last few years, I realized it is helpful to track what is done, what needs to be done, my plans, how an event goes, and other details, before, during, and after the event. Most conferences are clustered in Spring and Fall, so these times of year can be busy. This checklist helps me track details, so I can keep up with it all.

Speaking Engagements Checklist

Type of Event: _____ Date: _____ Time: _____
Organizer: _____ Topic: _____ Title: _____

Before

- ☐ Send title, description, bio, and headshot to organizer
- ☐ Update calendar in Gmail (Speaking Engagements, so it populates on website)
- ☐ Promote event when announced by organizer   unless Private Event
- ☐ Promote event: _____ _____ _____ _____ _____
  (month before, week before, day before)
- ☐ Complete slides
- ☐ Run Accessibility Check on slides
- ☐ Rehearse presentation
- ☐ Complete handout
- ☐ Questions During or After?

Plans

Date: _____   Time: _____
Notes:

During

- ☐ Note the following:
  Registrants: _____ Attendees (at start): _____
  Familiar folks: _____ _____ _____ _____ _____

After

- ☐ Send PDF of handout and/or slides to organizer
- ☐ Update website (Speaking Engagements page)
- ☐ Update LinkedIn (Public Speaker section)

Revised August 4, 2025   Courtesy of Kelly Schrank

STANDARD RESPONSE CHECKLIST

This is one of my medical communication checklists.

A standard response (SR), otherwise known as a standard response document (SRD) or standard response letter (SRL), is used by Medical Information in a pharmaceutical manufacturer when a health care provider calls their call center and asks for an answer to a specific question about a drug. A pharmacist answers the question verbally, often referring to the SR to do so. Then, if requested, they will fax or email the SR to the health care provider.

These are shorter documents, sometimes a couple pages, often six to eight pages, and rarely more than ten pages. Most companies have multiple SRs for each product, so a large manufacturer with multiple long-term products may have thousands of SRs, keeping editors busy on a full-time basis.

CHECKLIST EXAMPLES 113

Editor Checklist
Standard Responses

Instructions Use this checklist for US and Global SRs that need a standard edit.	
Owner: _____ Product: _____ Editor: _____	
Date Received: ___ Date Due: ___ Rush: Yes No SR#: _____	
Approve/Activate: Yes No Track Changes: Yes No # of Pages: ___	
Time: ___ ___ ___ Date Completed: ___ Entered in Tracker: ___ START STOP SPENT	
CHECK OUT DOCUMENT	
FORMATTING	
Turn on "Track Changes"	
Check SR Footer • Confirm that SR # is in footer. • If it is not, copy SR Document Number from **General Properties** and Paste Special into footer.	
Change Font Size of Normal Style to 11 pt	
Check/Correct Font Sizes in Document • Footer: 11 pt Times New Roman • Body text: 11 pt Times New Roman • Text in table/figure titles and in tables: 10 pt Times New Roman • Footnotes in tables/figures: 9 pt Times New Roman • References: 10 pt Times New Roman	
Check/Fix Justification Make sure body text, bullets, and references are left justified.	
Check/Fix "Keep with Next" near headings and tables (and within tables)	
Check/Fix Spacing in Bulleted and Numbered Lists Make sure bullets and numbers begin at the left margin and the tab is only .25" for each level. **Summary** Make sure this section has bulleted items, with 1 paragraph space between each bulleted item. (Make sure there are no paragraph spaces between sub-bullets.) **Clinical Data** Make sure there are no paragraph spaces between bulleted items.	
Check/Modify Headings and Sections of Document Look for consistency in heading levels, order of sections, and use of bullets.	

Heading Level 1	SR Sections (*Ex:* **Summary**; **Background**; **Clinical Data**)
Heading Level 2	Topic or Name of Trial (*Ex:* **Pharmacokinetics, The SAVOR Trial**)
Heading Level 3	Study Citation. (*Ex:* Wallentin et al. *N Engl J Med.* 2009;361:1045-1057.)
Heading Level 4	Topic: (*Ex:* Objectives, Methods, Baseline Patient Characteristics, Results)
Heading Level 5	Topic: (*Ex:* Design, Patients, Treatment Arms/Dosing, Primary Endpoint(s))
Heading Level 6	Topic

Check/Fix Spacing • Do a Find for a period followed by 2 spaces; replace with a period followed by 1 space. • Do a Find for 2 spaces within the text; replace with 1 space.

Editor Checklist
Standard Responses

ABBREVIATIONS	
Check/Fix Abbreviations and Acronyms	
• Make sure there are no periods in abbreviations. (*Ex*: ie, eg, US) (*Exception*: vs.)	
• Ensure that the composite words of abbreviations and acronyms are spelled out on first use in body text, followed by the abbreviation and/or acronym in parentheses. *Headings should have full version in most cases.*	
○ *Exception*: In some SRs, study name abbreviations and acronyms are used in summary bullets and spelled out on first use in the body of the SR.	
○ *Exception*: Some respiratory SRs use a legend at the beginning or end, so no abbreviations should be spelled out in the body of those SRs.	
• Use abbreviations and acronyms only if the term is used ≥3 times in the document. **Note:** If using *Find* and *Replace* to help locate abbreviations and acronyms, look for both the spelled-out versions ***and*** the abbreviations.	
• Make sure that abbreviations and acronyms are used consistently within the SR.	
CROSS-REFERENCES AND ENDNOTES	
Check/Format Cross-references and Endnotes	
• Count references; ensure they are in the correct order at first presentation.	
○ Generally, numbering starts in the Clinical Data section, not the Summary.	
▪ *Exception*: Background section may include references that are not used again.	
▪ *Exception*: Tables with details of studies might use endnotes, and study mentions thereafter in text would be cross-references, unless the studies are discussed in detail in text before mention in the table.	
• Make sure endnotes show references when you hover over them and that author names in body of SR match those in references (where applicable).	
• Make sure cross-references show a link when you hover over them.	
• Make sure all endnote and cross-reference numbers, ®, ™, and footnote symbols are superscript, without spaces between them and the word/data preceding them.	
• Make sure all endnote and cross-reference numbers are the same font size as surrounding text.	
TABLES/FIGURES	
Check/Fix Table/Figure Numbers in Text	
• Change any table/figure number mentioned in body text (*Ex:* "see Table I") to refer to the next table or figure (*Ex:* "as shown in the following table") where appropriate.	
• Count tables and figures; ensure tables and figures are numbered consecutively in bold capital Roman numerals. (*Ex:* **I, II, III, IV, V**)	
Check/Fix Table/Figure Titles, "Adapted from" lines, Endnotes/Cross-references, and Footnotes	
• Make sure "TABLE" and "FIGURE" are ALL CAP and bold. (*Ex:* **TABLE I, FIGURE II**)	
• Make sure a colon and 2 spaces follow the table/figure number, the table/figure title is **bold** and Initial Caps, and the title ends with a period. (*Ex:* **TABLE I: Title Title.**)	
• Ensure there is an "Adapted from" line (not bold) or an endnote/cross-reference after the title.	
• Ensure footnotes are indicated with superscript lowercase letters in alphabetical order (a-z) and that spaces are not superscripted.	

CHECKLIST EXAMPLES

Editor Checklist
Standard Responses

Check Table Formatting	
• Highlight each table:	
o Table Tools/Layout/Properties, ensure table is left aligned and the indent from left is .10″.	
• Make sure units of measure are specified in stub head, column headings, or row headings, but not duplicated in cells.	

Stub Head, n (%)	Column Heading	Column Heading	Column Heading
Row Heading			
Row Heading	Data in cell	xx (xx)	xx (xx)
Row Heading	xx (xx)	Data in cell	xx (xx)
Row Heading	xx (xx)	xx (xx)	Data in cell

• Make sure stub heads, column headings, or row headings and shaded rows match the following:
   o Text is **bold** and Initial Cap.
   o Stub head text is left justified and bottom aligned.
   o Column heading text is centered and bottom aligned.
   o Row heading text is left justified and center aligned.

• Ensure shading is correct: Ensure colors are used in correct order:
   • White, background 1, Darker 25% (third grey down, shown as selected in screenshot)
   • White, background 1, Darker 15% (second grey down)
   • White, background 1, Darker 5% (top grey)

• Make sure body cell text matches the following:
   o Text is sentence case and not bold.
   o Text is centered in cell (horizontally and vertically); text in left-most column is left justified and center aligned.
   o Bullets within tables are left-aligned and indented to half of the usual .25″ indent.

• If a table is very long and has to break between pages, ensure that header rows are repeated.

STYLE

Check/Fix Capitalization in Headings and Subheadings
Capitalize:
• Nouns, pronouns, verbs, adverbs, and adjectives; first word after a colon; first and last words
• Prepositions of ≥4 letters (*Ex:* With, From, Into, Onto)

Do NOT Capitalize:
• Articles and coordinating conjunctions (*Ex:* and, or, but)
• Prepositions of ≤3 letters (*Ex:* in, on, for)

Check/Fix Capitalization for Common Phrases
• Capitalize: Day 1, Week 1, Year 1, Phase III, **Note:**
• Do NOT Capitalize: stage IV, type 2 diabetes, grade 1

Check/Fix Numbers
• Use numerals to express numbers instead of spelling out the words.
• Numbers with >5 digits should have a comma. (*Ex:* 40,000; 400,000; 4,000,000)
• Always spell out numbers that begin a sentence; spell out ordinals. (*Ex:* first, second, third)

Check/Fix Units of Measure
Ensure the appropriate format of units of measure (ie, correct spacing between number and unit of measure).

Check/Fix Symbols and Signs
• Ensure the appropriate use and format of symbols and signs in body vs. within parentheses and in tables/figures. (*Ex:* virgule [/] should be "per" in body, but can be "/" in parentheses and tables)
• Make sure spacing before and after symbols is not superscripted).
• Spell out symbols and signs in text, except when used in lab values. (*Ex:* CK >10x ULN; HbA1c ≥6.5%; BMI ≥25 kg/m^2; sUA >6 [also, *target sUA >6,* but *sUA target goal of greater than 6*])

Editor Checklist
Standard Responses

REFERENCES
Check References Section:
- Ensure references are lined up on the left and the hanging indent is .13″.
- Make sure there are 2 nonsuperscript spaces after reference numbers 1-9 and between author(s) and reference titles.
- **Journal articles** should follow this example:
  Ando T, Ishikawa T, Kokura S, et al. Endoscopic analysis of gastric ulcer after one week's treatment with omeprazole and rabeprazole. *Dig Dis Sci.* 2008;53:933-937.
- **Web references** can be more complicated, but look for elements from the following example:
  Brown RW, O'Brien CD, Martin UJ, et al. Long-term safety and asthma control measures with a budesonide/formoterol pressurized metered-dose inhaler in African American asthmatic patients: a randomized controlled trial [published online ahead of print April 30 2012]. *J Allergy Clin Immunol.* 2012. http://dx.doi.org/10.1016/j.jaci.2012.03.028. Accessed February 15, 2013.

EDIT SR
Check for language usage issues:
- Adjust passive language to be more active, when possible.
- Replace jargon. (*Ex:* patient was on [medication] → patient received / was prescribed [medication])
- Make tense consistent. (*Ex:* in trial data, where tense changes)
- Use appropriate punctuation rules. (*Ex:* we use serial commas)
- Ensure that patients are discussed with respect. (*Ex:* replace "subjects" with a more appropriate term, eg, "patients," "participants," "recipients," "volunteers")

Common phrases that often need adjustment:

• "and colleagues"	• Change to "et al"
• "a total of"	• Delete, unless at start of sentence to replace long numbers
• "due to"	• Replace with "because of" in most cases (Note: due to = caused by)
• "respectively"	• Reword to eliminate, in most cases
• which vs. that	• Ensure words are used correctly
• "data" [singular verb]	• Replace with "data" [plural verb] (*Ex:* data were]
• "post"	• Replace with "after" when used as preposition
• "versus" or "vs."	• Use "versus" in body text and headings; use "vs." in tables and parentheses.

Turn off Track Changes (when necessary)

FINAL TOUCHES
Run Spell Check

Update Fields for Cross-references
Attempt to correct any "Bookmark not Defined" errors; if it's too complicated, ask author to correct.

Change View to 100% and Look Over SR One More Time
- Make sure tables break cleanly over pages and that column headings are repeated, as necessary.
- Replace hyphens and spaces in bad line breaks with nonbreaking hyphens or spaces.

Save Document

CHECK DOCUMENT BACK IN
Indicate what was done to the SR in the Description box. (*Ex:* Edited SR. Minor changes. OR Standard edit/tracked changes.)

Check Rendition in Viewer
- Open in Full Screen.
- Look for endnotes and cross-references coming in at a different size than the rest of the text or cross-references coming in not superscripted.
- Fix any issues, then re-upload a new version and repeat this step.

Editor Checklist
Standard Responses

	Complete the Task
	- Click **Complete**.
	  - *If you're in the Approval Cycle:*
	    - And the instructions were to edit and track changes:
	      - And other reviewers are included in the approval cycle: Click **Approved**.
	      - And NO other reviewers are included in the approval cycle: Click **Not Approved**.
	    - And the instructions were to edit and activate:
	      - And you have NO questions or tracked changes: Click **Approved**.
	      - BUT you have questions or tracked changes:
	        - And other reviewers are included in the approval cycle: Click **Approved**.
	        - And NO other reviewers are included in the approval cycle: Click **Not Approved**.
	  - *If you're in the Review Cycle:*
	    - Click **Approved**.
	- Click **Complete**.

	Notes **Find and Replace** **Great Catch!**

YOUTUBE VIDEO CHECKLIST

Crystal Herron shared this checklist that she developed for creating YouTube videos. She noted that she is still new to YouTube and experimenting with tools for creating videos, so the checklist is a work in progress.

YouTube Video Checklist

Title: _____

Post date: _____

Planning
- Craft title
- Craft thumbnail text
- Script opening
- Script closing
- Outline/script core
- Save script in Word
- Upload script/notes to PromptSmart

Video Recording
Lights
- Close desk curtains
- Hang 1 blackout curtain
- Turn on overhead lights

Camera
- Change cable
- Plug in back port
- Check Logitune
  - Turn off HDR
  - Change to 4K

Microphone
- Plug in front port
- Check placement in Zoom

PromptSmart
- Open script/notes
- Set microphone to Rode NT
- Size 24 font

Camtasia
- Project settings: 4K UHD 3840 x 2160, black background, 30 fps
- Camera setting: 3840 x 2160
- Microphone setting: Rode NT

Recording
- Test video recording
- Save file
- Check video not frozen

Video Editing
- Adjust project setting to 4K (not custom)
- Edit A-roll
- Import B-roll
- Add B-roll
  - Fade: 0:08
  - Drop: 0.20
  - Transition length: 3 s
- Add music
- Export audio
- Export video
- Save w/ SEO file name
- Review video

Record Timestamps
- _____ Intro
- _____ _____
- _____ _____
- _____ _____
- _____ _____
- _____ _____
- _____ _____
- _____ Outro
- _____ End screen

Closed Captions
- Upload file to transcription program
- Review captions
- Export as vtt
- Save w/ SEO file name

Thumbnail
- Take photo
- Import photo into Canva
- Create in Canva
- Download 1280 x 720
- Save w/ SEO file name

Description box
• Create description • Add affiliate links • Add links mentioned • Add references mentioned
Upload materials
Details • Upload video • Add title • Add description • Upload thumbnail • Add to playlist • Paid promotion: No • Altered content: No • Featured places: No • Automatic concepts: No • Tags: None • Recording date: None • Allow embedding: Yes • Allow remixing: No • Sort by: Top **Video elements** • Add subtitles (w/ timing) • Add end screen (video stage right) • Add cards **Visibility** • Public • Schedule (Fridays, 6:30 am)
Notes
Marketing
Newsletter • Add link and description **LinkedIn** • Create post • Schedule post **Academy** • Create post

ABOUT THE AUTHOR

Kelly Schrank, MA, ELS, is a seasoned technical writer and editor with over 30 years of experience across diverse industries and a medical editor in the pharmaceutical sector with 15 years of experience. As a **certified Editor in the Life Sciences**, Kelly has earned a reputation for precision, clarity, and expertise.

In 2011, a frustrating encounter with an ineffective editing checklist sparked Kelly's passion for improving checklists. What began as a personal project to refine her own checklists has since blossomed into a mission to **share best practices** with the wider medical communicator community.

Reach out with questions, coaching or speaking engagements, or collaboration opportunities: headbookworm.com

www.ingramcontent.com/pod-product-compliance
Lightning Source LLC
Chambersburg PA
CBHW060515030426
42337CB00015B/1898